Rudina Rexl

Freddie Mercury
Diary of a fan

Title | Freddie Mercury. Diary of a fan
Author | Rudina Rexhovaj
ISBN | 979-12-21488-92-0
Cover | Rudina Rexhovaj

© 2022 – All rights reserved to the Author
This work is published directly by the Author through Youcanprint self-publising platform and the Author holds all rights to it exclusively. No part of this book can therefore be reproduced without the prior consent of the Author.

Youcanprint
Via Marco Biagi 6 - 73100 Lecce
www.youcanprint.it
info@youcanprint.it
English Translation by Stefania Tavazzani

INTRODUCTION

"I think my songs can be classified as emotions. They have to do with love, passions and feelings. It's about moods. Most of the songs I write are love ballads and themes of sadness, suffering and pain, but at the same time they are frivolous and ironic."

Freddie Mercury – A life in his words

The need to express what I personally fell, prompted me to put on paper all the emotions and feelings I feel every time I listen to Queen's songs, interpreted by the unique and emotional voice of Freddie Mercury, with the hope of succeeding to pass them on to those who will devote their time to reading this book. Through this story, deeply felt internally, I would simply like to make known the reactions that such a powerful and penetrating voice unliashes. I would also like to make people understand the influence that such an eccentric character and extraordinary man had in my life and in that of the other fans, leading me to a change in my way of being and doing. I would like to make people understand what it means and what it feels like being a fan of him, what you do and the behaviors that result from it.

I'm not a writer, even if I like to write the thoughts of the moment on white sheets here and there, and I had so many of Freddie that I thought of bringing them together in a book composed by the voice of thoughts and heart, to share them together with the sentences of the other fans of the frontman, and leave them indelible over time. I express my emotions by talking about Freddie, but sometimes I feel the need to address him directly.

It is not my intention to dwell on the events of the band and even less on the statistics-dates, albums, concerts, live, but to tell my approach to Queen, my involvement and my experiences inherent to the band but especially to Freddie, and to bring to all the people who read this book the pleasant consequences that derive from listening to them by any means and at any time, and from visiting the places where they lived and composed their songs. And it is precisely there that the emotion multiplies. The extraordinary music and the content of the lyrics unleash emotions that accompany me in particular moments of life, and I would like to convey these emotions to the whole world, along with yours.

Freddie and you fans are my inspiration, and through these pages I would like to give a voice to all those who every day, even thirty years after his death, thank him for the legacy he left us, respect and love him, and write addressing him as if he were still alive, remembering him through songs, anecdotes, interviews, books, photos and numerous posts and links.

I would have liked to name you one by one, but for privacy reasons I limited myself to writing your thoughts at the end of each chapter. I'm sure that each of you will recognize his own words, and those that I have not been able to insert, will find themselves in the sentences written by the others, and in the thoughts that unite us. Always linking them to the title and content of each chapter, I introduced the phrases said by Freddie and the many translated verses.

There are many of us all over the world, we speak different languages but we understand each other anyway, because when it comes to Freddie the language becomes universal, when it comes to our Queen there are no distances or races, colors or religions. I won't repeat what we already know about our legend because it's not my place to do so. Many books have been written about him, and I think there isn't a fan who hasn't read again and again everything about Mr Mercury's life. I strongly wanted to show "the other side of the coin", that is me and those who follow him with passion: our thoughts, experiences, feelings and testimonies.

I try to describe and name the emotions I feel every time I listen to his songs, see a photo of him, hear his name and every time I watch a concert, a photo, an interview, a documentary about him. This book was born from the need to tell, explain and describe my life as a fan, how I approached this band and what I did for them, thus chronologically taking the nuances of a diary created with such devotion. I believe that every Freddie fan feels the same emotion that is shared on social media, and I hope that in this book they can find themselves in my words, as I found myself in theirs. I try to describe and name the emotions I feel every time I listen to his songs. I'm sure the phrases described by many people contain the thoughts and moods of everyone else. We express ourselves every day where we know we are understood and supported, and as a quick relay I would like to return the sensations that Freddie gives to me and to all of us, sharing them with other fans and not. We are truly an army of people and he is our suprem commander, we are sailors looking for a port and he is our captain. We are here anyway and everywhere for him.

"Queen's fans represent a very broad cross-section of society, and that's really good…it's nice that it's so diverse."

FreddieMercury – A life in his words
***

March 10, 2020

Two days ago, I was just in time to take the last plane back from abroad to Italy, just one day before all the borders were closed. We are living in an unusual reality and words like "pandemic" and "quarantine", in these modern time, seem new in the vocabulary. This involves physical closure, and dealing with it mentally is not easy.

We are not used to it, so we have to get busy in order not to fall into pessimism and despair, we have to cultivate and bring out our inner skills, whether they are reading, writing, music, painting, drawing, tailoring, cooking or other, all that can be achieved within the four walls. It's time to listen to ourselves, our needs, and come into contact with emotions, even the most hidden ones, seek and create ideas to develop and manage. For the first time we have so much time at our disposal and we have to make the most of it because this is the only way we will have a good memory of a bad moment. I think about my passions and I focus on the last one, reborn a short time ago: writing. I think about my compositions during my high school years with the highest of marks, the poems and lyrics I wrote a few years ago, and the idea of starting to put into practice my little talents inspires me to write this book as a memory of this period, but even more as the memory of a new passion.

At the beginning I thought that this lived experience would stay with me, but as I went on, I decided it would be nice to give my words to other people too, and also write their thoughts about the topic I wanted to discuss from my point of view, and this is how I would like it to be perceived, because emotions shouldn't be judged, but grasped in an empathetic way, making what belongs to others a little our own, and viceversa.

"Many people are creative in their own way. It doesn't have to be just in the music. This is also part of talent. I've always argued that you can't just sit at home and say, "Look how wonderful I am, I'm so creative, I'll wait." No. You have to go out there and grab it, you have to use it and make it work. That's part of talent."
                              Freddie Mercury – A life in his word

I introduce you my book-diary as a fan of Queen and in particular of Freddie Mercury.
Come with me on this beautiful journey through emotions!

BOHEMIAN RHAPSODY, THE MOVIE (2018)

"Besides, I have half a mind of a movie about my life. I could do it one day and have a key role, even if I don't necessarily have to be the protagonist:"
Freddie Mercury – A life in his words

1st January 2019 - Rome

It all started by chance at the end of December, when I was in Rome celebrating the New Year's Eve. After touring the whole city on a cool, dry Roman afternoon, with some friends we decided to go and see a movie. The advertisement had intrigued me about one in particular, and I immediately suggested it to the others. The cinema was located into a shopping center in the suburbs, so we took the ring road, fortunately quite smooth on that day of celebration. In bright sunlight, the plants looked greener and the leaves on the trees more orange. Caressed by its rays, I remained for a long time turned towards the slightly lowered window, lost in thoughts, absorbing the breeze that moved my hair, with my gaze towards nature. It felt like spring. I've always had a highly developed sixth sense, and the presentiment that I sensed allowed me to foresee a pleasant event, but I didn't think it would have pervaded my whole being in such an immediate way.

I felt the laughter and jokes in the car as if they came from afar, I was so relaxed and detached, but it was the sudden noise of braking that brought me back to my senses, and I heard the loud voice of the driver:

"Here we are guys, we have arrived at the *Gates of Rome*."

The mall was quite crowded. We headed for the cinema following the directions. There were many of us waiting in the hall, admists the murmur of people and the thin and joyful voices of the children who arrived.

Having only heard a few songs from this London band, I knew nothing of the musical career and even less of the private life of its members. The trailer of the film previously seen on television had attracted me a lot, and it was for this reason that I decided to see it. The line was quite long, even though the film had hit theaters in November. I could hear the people present interacting with each other:

"It's the third time I've seen it" said a middle-aged woman.

"Instead, for me it's the second one" replied a blonde girl, and while I was thinking about how good it would have been, since so many were there to watch it again, it was up to us to buy the tickets.

"Three tickets for *Bohemian Rhapsody*" we asked almost in chorus, and we burst out laughing at the pronunciation that wasn't the best. Not knowing the song, we couldn't get the peculiar English accent. After taking a selfie in front of the poster, we headed towards room 5, second side row on the right, with no possibility of changing seats, because it had sold out in a very short time. I thought that I would not have enjoyed watching the film properly, taking into account the proximity to the screen, but when the projection began I realized that from that distance it was as if I were next to this wild and attractive charactere, and if I had stretched out an arm I could have touched him.

The title, **Bohemian Rhapsody**, written in bold, rested on the broad shoulders of whoever composed that piece, as if to symbolize the great weight he would give to the history of music:

FREDDIE MERCURY.

Under a hot summer sun, the stream of people entering Wembley Stadium to the tune of *Somebody To Love,* seemed endless.

Find me somebody to love

> *Somebody, somebody, somebody*
> *Can anybody find me, somebody to love?*
> *Somebody To Love* (Queen, 1981)

Between the crunch of chips and popcorn, the room felt like a giant choir singing softly, and it was really exciting. It was impossible not to sing that refrain.

"What a charge this songs transmits!" I thought as I turned to look up at the mountain of people who filled the hall, admiring the uniqueness and spontaneity with which they participated. I turned over several times and as if by reflection, seeing all that crowd it seemed to me like I was attending a Queen concert and inevitably I said "Wow". The only difference was the number of attendance in the room. Never having been to a concert, I had never tried to sing my heart out with other unfamiliar people. And while these thoughts were going through my head, the image of the singer in jeans and a white tank top before the performance, who was hopping about getting ready to go on stage, made me experience a déja-vu. Two men in white shirts opened the curtain, but my desire to listen to the song to the end was interrupted by the automatic movement of the baggage carousel at Heathrow Airport in London. The year was 1970. A boy with medium-lenght black hair was staring at a suitcase, on which were written the names of several states. My simple interpretation fell on the desire to travel the world, when suddenly someone diverted my attention by calling him:

"Paki!"

"I'm not Pakistani" he replied without giving too many explanations.

Later someone from the crowd called him the same thing when he replaced the lead singer of Smile, Tim

Staffell. I thought it was a sign of contempt, but this time he began to sing lifting his chin and beating the tambourine hard on his thigh and on the microphone which, after trying to remove it from the support rod, suddenly detached. I felt annoyance towards whoever had uttered this epithet, and was particularly touched by this scene because it reminded me of when, at the same age, I was also an immigrant, and was often labeled in the same tone with my nationality of origin. Immersing myself in him, something strange that I will try to explain, happened to me: I felt kidnapped by this thin young boy with protruding teeth. His way of walking, his attitude, his very showy way of dressing, his deep gaze, the self-confidence he showed, aroused a lot of curiosity in me. I was particularly struck by his way of holding his head a little up, which at first glance seemed arrogant, but which instead was a sign of the height of his gaze, of his expectations and perspectives and of a projection into the future. He wanted to do what he did best: the performer, who gives people what they want.

The moment Freddie asked Brian and Roger to be their singer, I felt bitter again as the latter's answer: "Not with those teeth, man". I later discovered that fortunately it hadn't happened quite like that, but at the time that judgment based on external appearance annoyed me, making me empathize with this particular character.

Unlike someone esle who would have gotten angry, he so humbly made his voice heard by singing a short verse of *Doing All Right* (Smile, 1970):

I know what I'm doing
Gotta feeling I should be doing all right
Doing all right

… leaving both of them speechless and consequently me too, answering that he was born with four extra incisors, more space in the mouth, more vocal range. Ironically he turned and walked away, when asked

"Do you play bass?" he replied "No", and then left in a somewhat bizarre way.

He made me smile at the moment when I felt a little sorry for him. "What a strange and funny guy" I thought "he immediately puts you in a good mood".

The conflict he lived with his father helped him understand and implement the three main mottos of the Zoroastrian Parsi religion: "*Humata, Hukhta, Huvarshta*", that is "good thoughts, good words, good deeds", sending them back to him exactly before his contribution to Live Aid, and making him understand that there was nothing more useful than contributing to fight against hunger in the world. Without knowing if this scene had really happened, I was so touched by his embrace with dad Bomi.

I was enchanted by his love story. I found it out of the ordinary. Charming. He exuded a unique sweetness towards Mary, his girlfriend. The delicacy with which he asked her to marry him, with a jade ring depicting an Egyptian scarab, a symbol of resurrection (obviously I discovered this later) and the way he looked at her and said "You are beautiful", pronouncing the words from the bottom of his heart, they took my breath away. In that gaze there was everything: love, complicity, protection and dedication. His motto, *"You believe in me and I in you"*, at the moment of truth, of self-acceptance, made me understand that love can be lived in different ways, without completely losing the person you love, and at that precise moment I needed precisely this awareness.

The story of his life captivated me and I didn't want the film to end, or at least I wanted it to have a happy ending, even if it was impossible.

It was 134 minutes of pure energy. One of those "encounters" that change your life. That celestial voice struck emotional chords within me that I have never felt before. Many songs in the film, especially those from the 70s and 80s that I had never heard before, were a discovery.

Simply masterpieces and anthems, I was thrilled by the protagonist, or rather he, FREDDIE MERCURY. I had never felt such a strong emotional impact before.

I wondered why that thoughtful gaze directed through the window looking at who knows what, and with his back to everyone, when he heard the word *"Bismillah"*, mispronounced, *"Ismillah"*, by the record producer Ray Foster, known for let Queen escape, at least in the film. Perhaps he was looking at the path he had to take, but his answer amazed me again: "True poetry is for the listener." I was literally surprised by his answers, but the real poetry was him. And he continued to convince me of his determination with this answer:

"Ah! Don't get me wrong darling, it's going to be a rock and roll record, with the grandeur of opera, the pathos of Greek tragedy, the wit of Shakespeare, the overflowing joy of musical theatre. It will be a musical experience! It won't be just another record. Something for everyone, something people will find a sense of belonging in. We will mix genres, we will cross borders. We will speak unknown languages if we want."

Technically I don't understand much about music, but in that instant I understood that Freddie had an undisputed musical talent, and was a singer with a strong culture and a great passion for art, but especially for opera. The only singer who managed to weave rock with opera. I was amazed. It was simply BRILLIANT.

I felt great admiration as he sang *"Happy birthday to me, happy birthday mister Mercury"*, playing the piano and announcing to his family members his decision to change his name and surname at the registry office, saying that he never looked back, but only forward. He gave me the impression of a forward-looking person who was aware of what he wanted and how to get it.

However, returning to the darkness of room 5, fortunately no one could catch the crushed expression on my face. I was totally engrossed in his persistence and greatness, and couldn't take my eyes off Freddie, even though the other members of the band were on the screen as well.

Paradoxically, from a simple and silent place like a farm called Stocker Farm in Hertfordshire, in reality Rockfield Studios, between the mud and the crowing of a rooster, between the agricultural buildings and the immense greenery, one of the songs that made music history took shape. A solemn and absolutely innovative masterpiece, a musically perfect interweaving with a text that remains enigmatic even today, *Bohemian Rhapsody* (Queen, 1975).

"How was it possible that I had never heard such an excellent work as *Bohemian Rhapsody?*", I reflected incredulously. "What planet did I live on?". I was even ashamed to admit it. I, who couldn't live without music and did nothing but listen to it continuously, on the TV, from the cell phone, on the radio...perhaps they had stopped broadcasting Queen's songs, until the media impact of the film, which also ignited my desire to discover them. Many years ago I also wrote a poem, because...

With her I wake up and fall asleep.
Light, it caresses my hearing.
Like the same blood type.
It even enters my veins and gives me life.
Sometimes it takes the blame off.
From my guilty conscience.
It makes me relive my past.
So beautiful and blissful.
She is my best friend.
She is the music.

On the other hand, listening to their music was a surprise even for those who knew about it and for those who took advantage of it. But no one could stop them anymore: to the rhytm of *Now I'm here,* they began to realize the dream written on that suitcase at Heathrow Airport.

Now I'm here
Look around, around
Now I'm here
I'm just a, just a new man
Now I'm Here (Queen, 1974)

Queen began to conquer the entire planet. *"I am here"* said the first verse of that song, but they started to be everywhere: Denver, Portland, New Orleans, Atlanta, Pittsburgh, Edimburgo, Liverpool, Tokyo, Perth, Detroit, Glasgow, New York, Londra, Santa Monica, Boston, Osaka, Chicago, Sidney, Rio...
"Forced...twisted and meaningless"
"Nothing Memorable"
"Bad copy of Led Zeppelin"
"A pale reminder of the work"
"Queen are desperate to cement their seriousness"
"A song that should sink into oblivion"
"Bold jumble...pompous and too long"
"An attempt to mix at least six genres in six minutes."

These were just some of the comments of when *Bohemian Rhapsody* was broadcasted exclusively on Capital Radio 95,8 FM. Despite this, it seemed that Queen had made them the verses of Dante Alighieri: *"Don't worry about them, but look and pass over"*. In fact, Freddie Mercury says that Queen composed that single, one of a kind, at just the right time for that type of song.

However, a leader like him did not stop in front of prejudices, nor in front of disappointments. And the most tangible proof is his monologue to Paul Prenter (their manager for many years). A slap to all those who had betrayed him or tried to exploit him for his fame. Those strong words have remained etched in my memory:

"I want you out of my life. I blame myself. Do you know when you realize you've become rotten to the bone? Gnats, nasty little gnats come to feed on the leftovers. Well, I'm sorry for you, there's very little left to eat. So now fly away and do whatever you want with your photos and your stories, but promise me one thing: I'll never see your face again. Never again."

And he left in the rain under the notes of *Under Pressure,* as only sincere souls can do.

Pressure pushing down on me
Pressing down on you no man ask for

Under Pressure (Queen and David Bowie, 1981)

That moment made me feel sad for Freddie, and sorry for the other. I immediately understood his being a special person, in need of love, born with an altruistic nature, different from the character he played on stage. And even when he got carried away, he managed to find the strength to react, demonstrating it even in the face of a ruthless fate.

With background music from *Who Wants to Live Forever?* Freddie entered the clinic. The rhythm of the notes followed his steps that seemed to lead, synchronized with the beats of my heart. The doctor's incomprehensible words in the background music, the imaginable diagnosis, my indescribable displeasure and the salty taste of tears that flowed like a raging river caused the flood.

There's no chance for us
It's all decided for us
This world has only one sweet moment
Set aside for us

Who Wants to Live Forever? (Queen, 1986)

His strength in dealing with the news of the disease, and the way he communicated it to other Queen were admirable: he was the one who tried to give support to others, and at the same time announced that he could still give the best of his music.

With the start of *Live Aid*, the film had come to an end. The hours had flown by among songs and jokes, dialogues and monologues and my torments about how this would end. The performance was thrilling. On stage, Freddie was unattainable with his performance, with his *"Eeeeoooo"*, the roar of the lion that dominates the crowd, which in turn respondend with the same *"Eeeeoooo"* in unison. As our star said, "They believe in you and repeat the same gesture as in the Olympics".

It started with *Bohemian Rhapsody* and Freddie, as promised, blew a kiss to his mum. After the last song, *We Are the Champions*, he also did it with the audience, and then bowed, a sign of his humility and respect fot the fans, while Mary had teary eyes. As he turned in slow motion to the other members of the group, he seemed to be turning to the audience in the cinema, and then triumphantly exited. He, the undisputed champion. After him came John, and finally Brian and Roger together, just like in reality. Freddie left planet Earth, John the stage, and for Brian and Roger the show continues.

I seemed to be inside the screen, among the thousands of people who filled Wembley, with all the emotions that one experiences at a concert, feeling a volcano inside me, the magma that burned and came out following the eruption. Pure energy. Thrills and endless admiration for the greatest frontman of all time. I didn't know how to give a name to what I was feeling, or maybe I should have invented it and asked the Accademia della Crusca if it could be accepted. A mix of infatuation, falling in love, adrenaline, passion. Between losing your mind and losing touch with reality. I just know that feeling was amazing.

Just like in the Olympics, even though they didn't win any medals, they were the undisputed champions. Eighteen minutes of enchantment that will remain the most beautiful in the history of music. Freddie gave off a vitality that was reflected in all faces, but above all in that son who embraces his father, excited to relive that moment (actually he had been present at Live Aid 1985).

I too was eager to see the real Freddie, who appeared dressed in black leather, with the full band, singing *Don't Stop Me Now*. I devoured him with my gaze while the notes of the music revolved around me in the space that remained inside that bubble I had created. I felt alive.

"Don't stop me now... I don't want to stop at all, Mr Fahrenheit"

From the power of the voice it seemed that the walls were shaking and the surround effect amplified everything, making the performance more enveloping. With the black screen in the background and the end credits rolling upwards, my face was once again wet with tears as *The Show Must Go On* began with the words *The end*.

I hadn't taken into account that soon I would have lived in another dimension that would have changed my way of life. I sat for a while as everyone left. Evidently I didn't want to leave someone or something precious that I had found in that cinema at the *Gates of Rome*, but which for me was like *Nuovo Cinema Paradiso,* and just like Giuseppe Tornatore's film it taught me to dream the impossible, and that anything can be achieved, just like Freddie did. So I decided to take him with me. His every movement, every expression, every gesture, not to mention his crystalline and at the same time powerful voice, which that evening conquered every pore of my body reaching up to my soul. It started with *Find me somebody to love...* and I ended up finding it. I found someone to love, without if and but, without complications and expectations, without demands and interests, requests and contacts. And all this could be called love at first sight: I was electrocuted, with invisible signs hidden inside. A part of me remained in the second row with trembling breath and the feeling of disconnection from reality, and the other part brought with it that music that knows how to excite.

Unknowingly the desire arose in me to see the film again, two, three, more times, whether the screening was in English or Spanish, whether it was in the karaoke version, it didn't matter because by now I knew the lines by heart, until I lost count. Even if this attitude didn't seem normal to someone, for me it was like listening to a a song over and over again, because you like it and because at that moment you can't live without it. And I should truly thank the actor Rami Malek for having interpreted his important role in such an original way, because it is thanks to him and the other actors that I approached the music of Queen and their story.

***

At first I thought I was the only one to suffer Freddie's timeless charm, so much so that I tried to mask the sparkle in my eyes and the smile that inevitably arose when talking about him, but luckily I was wrong. I was not the first, let alone the last, to whom the Freddie Mercury effect had caused a similar attraction, as the comments of these fans demonstrate.

"In 2018 the film Bohemian Rhapsody *was released in all theaters and from there I met you. Before I only heard your name, but since I saw the film I've known your story, and you entered me and you will never come out again. I have no words to describe you, I just say thank you for existing."*

"About a year ago I discovered Queen. One could say "You've only known Queen for a year? How is it possible? The truth is that knowing them has a meaning, discovering them another. Everyone knows and hums Queen's biggest hits, and up until a year ago I was one of them too. But discovering Queen instead means being

hungry for information, experiencing them deeply, getting excited about the anecdotes of their lives, examining the photographs, imagining being at one of their concerts and above all appreciating songs that I would never have known if I hadn't decided to truly discover Queen."

"No consegui acreditar no que vi a primeira vez que assisti o filme. (vi 28 vezes no cinema e outros miles em casa). Me emocionou muito, chorei boa parte do filme. Eu tinha visto Queen so vivo no Rockinrio'85 e cambio minha vida para sempre. O filme me trouxe Queen e Freddie de volta! Eu tinha brigado com a música quando perdi meu filho em 2001 com 22 anos. Era músico, guitarrista e compositor. A partir do filme voltei a ouvir e ver Queen. Estão na minha vida novamente. Me devolveram à vida! (Sem falarque a atuação do Rami me comoveu profundamente)". *"I can't believe what I saw the first time I watched the film (I've seen it 28 times at the cinema and a thousand more at home) I was very emotional, I cried for a good part of the film. I saw Queen live at Rock in Rio '85 and it changed my life forever. The movie brought back Queen and Freddie to me! I had fallen out with music after losing my son in 2001 at the age of 22. I was a musician, guitarist and composer. I'm back in my life. They brought me back to life! (not to mention that Rami's performance deeply moved me)"*

"it made me think, where was my brain when this man was alive? I'm so saddened that I was old enough to enjoy his existence, but chose not to worry about it (it was kinda weird to be honest, but rock music was only for bandits!). Only after the film did I become a big fan now in my maturity. I was totally blown away by the sex God he looked like! Well, better late than never. That I missed, I would like to have met him or even just be able to say that I have seen him live. Today I am 53 years old."

"Beautiful! I've seen it at least 15 times and every time you always perceive something new, and the more I

watch it the more it seems that Freddie is still physically here with us. Always an emotion, always in our hearts, and I think that, although he didn't look much like him in the face, Rami was very good. In the movements he was identical."

"I first saw it in English in April on the plane to Bangkok on my honeymoon. An indescribable emotion, which powerfully rekindled the never extinguished flame of passion for Freddie. We spent 10 days on the beaches of Thailand listening to his songs. I'm 42 and the memories of Queen and Freddie were a bit distant after so many years, the film made them come alive in an istant. Freddie I miss you."

"Although due to their age I could have followed them as a girl, I haven't had anyone in my family or friends who talk about them. I followed many singers, radio and TV programs but hardly anything from Queen. A few songs, but not passed that often. The film: a revelation! Okay, he may not have been faithful to the story, but he gave the incentive as I think to all the others who found out from the film, to know more about Queen and Freddie Mercury!"

***

But of course most fans discovered them many, many years ago, some from the beginning of their careers. Here are some of their testimonials.

"My passion was born when I was a little girl. My brother listened to various rock music including Queen and as soon as I heard Bohemian Raphsody *it was love at first listen and I stole his cassette. After a while* Living On My Own *came out and it was the years of full discos and that music took me completely."*

"Mine was born way back in 1984 at Sanremo Festival."

"I was little, about 10/11 years old when I heard Radio Ga Ga *for the first time. They played it a lot on the*

radio, and I loved that music. I've always listened to them ever since."

"My passion was born when I was 11 listening to Bohemian Rhapsody *on the radio, then after a short time I saw the video for the first time. Since then, there's only Freddie for me."*

"He burst into my heart during Sanremo in 1984, and he's still there. I love him madly. Freddie was unique, histrionic, extravagant, courageous, beautiful."

"The first time I listened to Queen was in 1989. The Miracle had just come out. I was literally electrocuted and have loved their music ever since. I took breaks during my path but nothing captivates me like when I listen to them, I've only seen the film four times and I have to say it's done well."

"I was 4 years old and my dad always made me listen to this tape in the car. From there it was love. I still have that tape."

"I've been following him for a lifetime and my children have grown up with his music. Unique Freddie."

"Just think that I've been following Queen and him."

"Freddie entered my heart in the early 70s and never came out."

***

"We certainly don't want to abandon our old fans who have been following us since the beginning and are always there, (at least I hope so) but we also want to attract a new audience."

Freddie Mercury – A life in his words

Honey, you're starting something deep inside of me
Honey, you're sparking something, this fire in me
Breakthru (Queen, 1989)

THE AFTER FILM

"We were perfect strangers, and out of the blue we were on top of the world."
Freddie Mercury – A life in his words

Each of us expects something beautiful and overwhelming to happen in our lives sooner or later. A great love, a marriage proposal, a son, an unexpected trip, a surprise birthday, or maybe an unpredictable meeting. One of those that change your life, that give you the strenght to go on, and the peace of mind that you longed for, one of those full of emotions already hidden somewhere that catch the wind and take you far away. Just what happened to me, after discovering Freddie Mercury and Queen. It was from amazement that the discovery of their story began.

Thirsty to know more and more, I started looking for more information about Freddie's life and Queen's career. The curiosity to know every aspect that concerned him, was like a spiral that sustained me uninterruptedly in my research, and the interest that arose from learning something new increased day by day. I watched the film several times, and tried to find the titles of all the songs in the soundtrack. I downloaded them and listened to them all the time, as they were "new" songs to me, never heard before. I read many books, biographical and otherwise, in order to enter his majestic world, that of worldwide success of a singer, but also in his personal one. His music and the harmony among Queen's voices were so overwhelming that I couldn't help but listen to them incessantly.

The songs of the 70s were an immense discovery. *Killer Queen, White Queen, Now I'm Here, Seven Seas of Rhye, The March of the Black Queen, The Fairy Feller's Master-Stroke, Father to Son, In the Lap of the Gods, Dear*

Friends, Get Down Make Love, and many others became my favorite. By day, by night, with headphones or at high volume, those songs accompanied me in my daily life, and their lyrics flowed like a cascade of water which, upon impact with the soul, made a thunderous and surprising noise, and the sound sometimes sweet, sometimes impetuous thrilled me. Freddie's voice, so clear and at the same time so influential, entered my veins, so much so that I was completely addicted to it. There were many emotions I felt since MY MESSENGER OF THE GODS, MERCURY, entered my life. I imagine him proud as he decided: "I want to call myself Mercury, because the mother of that song is my mother.

> *Mother Mercury, Mercury*
> *Look wat they're done to me*
> *I cannot run, I cannot hide*
>
> *My Fairy King* (Queen, 1973)

Someone was daze by what happened, someone took me for crazy, someone told me that I suffer from erotomania (using this label improperly, probably without even knowing the true meaning of the word), and someone simply showed incomprehension, but there are also those who have understood me and supported me by saying "If it makes you feel good, keep following it", and those who have been able to welcome this new passion. Precious gifts such as T-shirts, DVDs, books and other gadgets were always a very pleasant surprise for a newbie like me.

"You're obsessed" they told me, but without that "obsession" I couldn't live any longer. "You have to take care of yourself" they told me, but if that was a disease, I didn't want to get better. If they told me I was going to be such an avid fan, I would have believed it. When I watched fans of other singers or other bands screaming, crying and fainting at their idols' concerts, I thought they were exaggerated. Those heart-rending screams and singing at the top of their lungs seemed like a set-up to me.

Nowadays, however, I think that one should never judge before trying, but during my youth, empathy was not a feeling that belonged to me. I was struggling to understand certain attitudes and their way of showing their presence. For sure, due to the character I have, I wouldn't have pulled my hair out, but if I had seen him live, I don't know how I would have reacted. Or maybe yes...I would have screamed his name, I would have waited hours to see him even from afar, I would have cried and they would have been nothing but tears of pure joy and who knows...I would have certainly wanted an autograph, a photo, a hug...if...I knew that all of this would never happen, but I imagine that I would have been satisfied with being a dot in that oceanic crowd just to see once, just once, even from a distance, his eyes made up with eyeliner.

  I was experiencing an intense feeling of affection towards Freddie, through which I began to love myself more, to dream, to dare more than before, arriving at increasing my inner growth. And when they asked me "How do you have such feelings for a person who is no longer there?" I replied: "No one dies as long as he lives within us, as long as he makes us live". Freddie is more alive than ever. His greatness dominates our minds. He's present and he's within us. He's life.

  I had good sensations and despite everyday problems, it seemed to me that I faced them more lightly. Queen songs accompanied me throughout the day. Freddie was so explosive and exuberant that he kept me stuck into a reality made of a very pleasant creative work that led this band to be one of a kind. Theirs was another music, the one that I had never known enough until now, the one that had not yet caressed my hearing, when I saw his fingers glide across the piano keyboard in the most exorbitant way I've ever seen. I compared him to Mozart, and when his beautiful hands gripped the microphone with such dedication, accompanied by his sensual contortion, I gasped.

You Take My Breath Away (Queen, 1976). You take my breath away, dear Freddie.

On the other hand, how can you not be struck by the genius of this star that shines more than the others? It illuminates you with all its splendor and becomes a thread of light that shows you the way. The emotions I felt had no logic, no reason, much less an explanation. They came overwhelming me completely. They didn't knock before entering, making me leave aside the kind of music I was listening to before: classical, jazz, blues, trip-hop and hang, to give space to Queen, the most eccentric and glamorous rock band that I had ever seen. It amazed me how after so many years their songs sounded so current. And so, I became a fan of a band with a capital B as they say, but for its lead singer I just lost my mind.

Somebody say that the film has "divided" the fans, with pros and cons, but in my opinion it has also united them. It was a turning point for my life, and I know that even if it was criticized for its inconsistencies and inaccuracies (I think the authors did it consciously), it still reawakened the passion for a band that made history of music. I always see the bright side of things. The army of old fans has been joined by the kids of the new generation and not, and personally I am part of the latter. I'm a new fan, but that doesn't take away from the intensity with which I follow Queen, and I assure you it's the same as that of the older ones. And apart from everything, the most beautiful thing was uniting people from all over the world in the name of four guys who have played an important part in the history of music, John, Brian, Roger, but above all the one who invented his character, Mr Mercury, the one who like no other knew how to get in full harmony with the audience. The rest has been proved by the course of events.

***

"Of course I'd like everyone to say that I'm wonderful and that they love my songs."
Freddie Mercury – A life in his words

You've captured my love
Stolen my heart
Changed my life
I'll be right behind you -
Right until the end of the earth
I'll get no sleep till I find you to tell you
That you just take my breath away
*You Take My Breath Away (*Queen, June 15, 1986)

FREDDIE AT THE TIME OF SOCIAL

"When success comes, it's the fans who decide whether it has to be like this or not.."

FreddieMercury – A life in his words

I wonder that it would have been like to go and see Freddie Mercury's profile on various social networks. What he would have written, the photos he would have posted, the performances directly from his home, Garden Lodge, the tours...I imagine him live in front of the piano singing new songs.

It would have been great, Freddie, to write you directly and wait for a reply from you, or even just listen to you again. Obviously I'll never know what I would have felt, but I can imagine.

After discovering Queen, and while I was collecting news on various sites about Freddie's life, the idea of looking for groups dedicated to him on social network didn't immediately occur to me, but after a few months, when I discovered them, a world unknown before then opened up to me. The world of Freddie fans on social media is a world unto itself. It looks like a sea in continuous movement, in which the highest wave follows the one directed towards the shore: a post followed by comments, a photo with emoticons, a live by gifts. Populated by people from all over the world, it becomes full of colors, stories, different languages, passion, common but also contrasting thoughts, comparison and sharing. I became aware of many groups and pages all over the world, called with names that evoked the title of a song, a verse, a word or simply his name.

Administrators of several groups and members greeted me with a welcome, a heart, or brief welcoming comments. It was understandable that I was one of them, that I loved Queen, that I was in love with Freddie, that I shared the same crazy passion, and that I understood them without judging, it felt like being inside a big family, in which the good morning was not given around the breakfast table, but on a virtual bulletin board, with a phrase dedicated to our prince, or to the whole band, through a song or a photo. There was no better way to start the day and continue it, because the administrators of the group are a bit like mums, who find the time to organize everything and keep you busy throughout the day with contests for the cover, information about the band, photos, perhaps organizing a video party in the evening, a moment where all together, as if we were sitting on a sofa next to each other, with a can of Pepsi or a cup of tea, we could watch a concert, applaud via emoticons, comment with the sweetest words, hearts and the likes that flew up until they disappeared. And we women, mothers, wives, girlfriends, or singles, but also many men and boys, for a moment we went back to happy and carefree teenagers.

So the ability to use communication began to be part of the universal law of giving and receiving, strengthening these social ties, coming to feel gratitude, always thanking those who did something for us instead of taking it for granted, the groups had an energizing effect, and were a place of information with different subjects that allowed for exchange, they facilitated the meeting among people who knew each other only virtually, giving positive effects, the dynamics that were created had pleasant and shared effects, and we became a large extended family in which all generations were involved.

At first I thought that Cupid had only hit me, but I realized I wasn't the only one, so I joined many others old and new lovers who, unlike other "polygamous loves", ironically speaking, they lived in peace and harmony. The difference among fans of other singers and fans of Freddie lies in the fact that their idols are still alive (obviously not all), instead we feel a bit orphaned by Freddie. While they follow the news of events, new concerts coming up, a new record, fresh news, many of us cling to the past of Queen as a whole, a past that is very present. Sometimes a demo version, a piece of a video never seen before or an unpublished photo generate happiness. Comments like *I've never seen this picture before, or When did you wear this hat?* arose curiosity and the novelty seems to topical that it happened the same day. It impresses us and fills our eyes.

***

JANUARY 2020

"It's not easy to create a group from scratch. You would llike to share and shout your love for Freddie with people who can understand you. And when you realize that everyone is serene and harmonious inside the family, then your heart opens up with joy because Freddie guides and inspires us. Thanks to all of you who have helped me make this a fantastic group."

"It is an harmonious group in which one perceives only the great love that binds each of us to our immense Freddie."

"Thanks from me too! I feel like family with you sharing your love for Freddie!"

"We share the intent and joy of celebrating, remembering, perpetuating and loving Freddie, and that's a wonderful thing.

***

11 April 2020 at 10:38 am

"A year ago I joined this wonderful group. There are so many emotions that drive me to write these lines, but above all having discovered new and very interesting things about my favorite singer and his group: Freddie Mercury and Queen, despite the fact that I have been following them since 1980 and I am well supplied of books, records, cds, whs etc. sometimes you need to know more and more, and this is exactly where I found it all. That's

why I thought I'd thank all of you for what you tell us for better or for worse, through the posts of you admins and moderators, and all the other members of the group. We never learned enough, so even if sometimes we seem to be missing for a while without publishing posts or anything else, we're always there, maybe in the shadows, but we're here, because the desire to know and discover new things it's huge

, so once again thanks team for existing!

"It's a great group, the news is always relevant and well rated. Thank you for the company you always keep us and especially at this moment."

"Yesterday a reflection I made was:"Yes, it's true, I recorded all the documentaries, but do you want to watch them, knowing that all over Italy others like me, lifelong fans, are watching it at the same time?". An evening seemingly alone."

***

Sometimes a photo or a sentence is enough to receive synthetic answers expressed through adjectives in return. Comments are always followed by different emoticons, hearts of all colors, smileys with hearts, stars, sun, cats, roses, microphones, keyboards, headphones, CDs, music staves, applause, and the King's crown is inevitable. All that brings us to Freddie and Queen.

January 7, 2020

A fan posts a photo of Freddie with his fist raised in front of a crowd and writes:

The God of crowds. The one who was able to hold thousands of people in his grip with his talent, his charisma, his being. Freddie Mercury.

The others follow it with these words:

"The world at his feet."

"A wonderful picture: his unique grit and the audience leaning towards him."

"A great one, for sure. One is born every thousand years."
"You can feel his charisma and ability to interact with the public."
"Beautiful!!!"
"Marvelouos."
"A God worshiped by the crowd."
"Empathetic always."
"Omnipotence."
"You look like A God, Freddie!"
"Unforgettable."
"Great frontman."
"And his voice...unique."

***

For us fans, expressing ourselves through epithets and metaphors means amplifying the content of the concept, with the aim of attributing particular characteristics, arriving at different nuances, creating new unions and recalling emotions, to inspire joie de vivre through another language. Symbolizing Freddie with the four elements of nature, essential elements for life, means that for us he is still part of life, that he lets us live and is indispensable for us. To me Freddie represents water, both salty and fresh. The liquid matter par excellence, the genesis of life, the natural and indispensable element.

On stage he is an ocean wave, capable of overwhelming thousands of people with his unmistakable *"Eeeeeoooo"* which drags you ashore with his size, making you feel a thrill, and when he is off stage he is water calm of a transparent lake sweet and quiete. Over the years, his metamorphosis is comparable to the same material, water, but in different forms: ice, limpid and crystalline like his voice, dense like an iceberg which sets out to protect the underlying water from freezing, showing only a part of itself, the one that resists the sun's rays, but in depth it manifests itself with triple the proportions hiding fears, loneliness and the search of affection, and when it falls it turns into soft snow that protects the ground from frost, as Freddie protected those around him.

***

January 2020. An admin of a group writes:

"What element of nature does Freddie make you think of? And why? I associate him with the moon, so changeable, so luminous, and then dark, almost hidden. Round and perfect when full, other times a slice sensually resting on the sky. Freddie, my satellite."

The other fans respond like this:

"What a beautiful post! I associate him with the wind. Many times a breeze that passes lightly through your hair, sometimes strong that takes you where it wants, and enters you upsetting your soul, and then leaves you there dazed to think about which emotion has upset you the most."

"I associate him with the sun and fire, for the energy he releases, for the warmth of the great love of his deep heart, combined with the yellow color he loved so much. And I am a sunflower that revolves around you, that are my sun even at night. *Water air fire light dark...I add earth as an element of complete conquest!"*

"My darlings, you have chosen all the elements and left me with no choice but to join them all together for Freddie is, indeed, in perfect harmony and balance with each. He is a true child of the forces of Nature".

"Well, Freddie to me can only be one element: fire. Just look at him. He was fire when he was on stage, he set the audience on fire. Fire as he moved like crazy. My fire when I see him..."

"Freddie reflects many elements of nature, he is multifaceted. Fire because it is volcanic, the sea calm or agitated like his character, the moon romantic and melancholy, the earth because he was stubborn and

Mercury the messenger of the Gods. His message went straight to the heart, soul and brain. P.S. I also added planets.

"I think he represents all the elements when understood as fire, air, earth and water. The continuous evolution of fire, the spirit of air and its ability to infuse the soul, the earth as a primordial material from which everything began, water and birth and rebirth. For me Freddie is all of this. And all of this is Love in whatever form you want to see it."

"You are the sun that warms my heart. I think about you 23 hours and 59 minutes a day, and in that other minute I think it's good to think about you."

***

While the sun hangs in the sky and the desert has sand
While the waves crash in the sea and meet the land
While there's a wind and the stars and the rainbow
Til the mountains crumble into the plain
Oh, yes, we'll keep on tryin'
Innuendo (Queen, 1991)

***

The testimonials and words these fans write need no comment. They speak for themselves, with the voice of truth and love for Freddie. And everything that is written comes from the heart in the most sincere way, and consequently they let themselves go to bring out the best of their thoughts and emotions, describing the details, using irony and the most appropriate adjectives for him. Brian says Freddie wanted to make an intimate connection with his audience, and it was mutual, because we also make that same connection with him, which allows us to see not only the character but also the exquisite person he was. The group belongs to an ideal that for us is Freddie, and we keep it active through the words that lead to it, with the aim of keeping it alive. The spell that Freddie has created over us is like a common thread that binds soul mates from birth and the bond is inseparable, that fil rouge that carries the love we show towards him. If we could see him, it would make us think that he binds the most unthinkable and apparently distant people, who share everything about his career and his life in privacy.

I thought: on the basis of that criteria do we choose to form a subgroup that links people at a distance, people who basically don't know each other? I was thinking of the hidden world of fans, what you do not see and hear in front of everyone, the numerous sub-groups and the freedom of expression in absolute privacy, the bond that is formed, knowledge and how these previously unknown people become so familiar, so close to each other that they seem like sisters and brothers. There is communication and a daily exchange among us, but often I also feel the need to address Freddie directly. Even if you couldn't live social media time, I'm sure that from up there you read everything we write about you every single day. Even if so many years have passed, and still more years will pass, there will always be someone who will listen to your music and who will describe the emotions you give us every time your voice pierces our hearts.

***

Many have dreamed of him and many are waiting to. I dreamed of Freddie four times, but I remember the first dream well and I would like to tell you about it.

I was in the courtyard of my school (the pedagogical hig school), walking with my best friend Eda, dressed in a black tunic with a white collar (uniform was a must), and I had just received the news that Queen were stay in the hotel across the school (actually there were only houses). I remember accelerating my steps towards the high wall that divided it from this phantom hotel, and looking impatiently towards the terraces. At one point, I saw Freddie waving me up. I ran after his invitation and found myself in his room. There were also Brian, Roger and John, who I greeted without stopping to join Freddie on the terrace. He kindly pulled a chair up to me, put a cushion on it, and waited for me holding it until I sat down. We looked at each other and started talking (I don't remember in which language), making jokes and laughing as a result. After that we got into a car, destination unknown...

I woke up with an indescribable feeling of well-being pervading my mind and body. I would also have gone to heaven with you, Mr Bad Guy, to collect rainbows in the sky, it would have been enough to ask me: Oh spread your wings and fly away with me".

Wish my dream would never go away -
Barcelona (Freddie Mercury and Monserrat Caballé, 1988)

Having attended the Gestalt Counseling institute, I was reminded of the meetings about the meaning of dreams, and the importance of recognizing through them the shortcomings of which we are not aware and which, once identified, we try to address. The meaning of dreams is a very intriguing topic, because the content can be so inexplicable, fascinating and compromising that it leaves an emotional influence for a long time after we wake up. The way I recounted my dream, the tone of voice and the emphasis, it was as if I was reliving it again in that moment.

When we dream we are so involved that the dream seems like reality. Through the story it is if we were resurrected, giving importance to the details which, once put together, help us to give meaning and could help us to arrive at an awareness. What we dream can affirm what we desire. With dialogue we unknowingly trust our shortcomings and our needs, and this is reflected in my dreams, but I think it is reflected in those of each of us.

The interpretation of this dream fell on the fact of not having known Freddie before, in adolescence, and the laughter that inevitably occured in the other two dreams, in addition to the complicity, highlighted our very satirical and friendly characters.

In any case, the dream, like passion and music, becomes a therapy for the soul, and Freddie has become our trusted "psychologist".
There are dreams with closed eyes and those with open eyes. The latter to enter the Duck House one day with other fans to share the experience and to imagine him, even briefly, in his environment, imaging him sitting there in that chair making fun of all the ducks that were everywhere in the house, that for this reason he nicknamed "Duck House". Who knows if I would have heard his good laugh and felt the lightheartedness of the early years, I thought. I wanted to relive his creativity and see the places where he was inspired to compose his music. I was planning more trips to the places where Freddie spent his time making music, to see the houses where he lived, the recording studios, the concert venues and the restaurants and pubs he frequented.
We fans come from all over the world. Everyone has his own life, his family and job, but everyone is always available to cut out a piece of the day to dedicate to Freddie and Queen. The group keeps us busy and always with a new expectation, a new idea that keeps us connected, fills us with the joy of waiting, another goal. We also need this in life. Our motto is inspired by a title of a song by Queen, *Teo Torriatte*, that is "let's stick together" or "let's hold each other" as Freddie interprets it. Whatever the true translation, the sense remains the same.

***

You brought me fame and fortune
And everything that goes with it, I thank you all
We Are the Champions (Queen, October 7, 1977)

"I am very happy doing what I do. In a way I feel obligated to the fans. What's more important than me is the audience."

Freddie Mercury – A life in his words

MONTREUX

The multiple information learned from various books led me to know the places where Freddie had lived, and the ones he was most fond of: Zanzibar, Bombay, Panchgani, London, Montreux, Munich, New York, Japan, and the idea of going to visit them came to me by default, without knowing that by now the statue of Freddie, created by the Czech artist Irena Sedlecká in his memory, had become a pilgrimage destination for fans from all over the world.

May 19, my fiftieth birthday, was about to arrive and I decided to make it memorable. Having attended the linguistic high school, it was also a good opportunity to brush up the French language and set the reservation mechanism in motion: train, Hotel, restaurant and pastry shop, where I ordered a cake with a 3D image of Freddie. A few phone calls to friends, and I started organizing everything. Time was short, a weekend. I wanted to see every place, every object, everything to do with Freddie and Queen. I wanted to breathe him. I couldn't wait for all of this to happen. My heart was in my throat and I didn't sleep a wink that night.

18 May 2019 at 6:20 am

The fateful day arrived, and with it a thousand mixed emotions gave me a sense of euphoria. Freddie's voice accompanied me for most of the journey and as I listened to *A Winter's Tale*, I imagined myself already there. Only those who have experienced this sensation can understand me. From the headphones, Freddie's voice came clear and blissful.

It's all so beautiful
Like a landscape paiting in the sky
Am I dreaming?
A Winter's Tale (Queen)

"Prochain arret, Montreux" announced the railway clerk.

I was about to set foot in the country that attracted the father or romanticism Victor Hugo, the actor and film producer Charlie Chaplin, the symbolic writer of the twentieth century Ernest Hemingway, the Enlightenment Jean Jacque Russeau and perhaps, given the influence he had on him, also the writer Nicolaevic Tolstoy and many others, but above all the greatest performer of all time, Freddie Mercury.

In front of me for the first time the Montreux Riviera, overlooking the splendid Lake Geneva and the majestic Alps, looked like a postcard, and the blue-gray colors filled my eyes, making the scene surreal. Finding myself in the midst of a few passers-by who were walking towards the shore, I quickened my pace towards the statue. My heart was pounding, because to me that statue contained a soul, a heart and a mind. It was Freddie clad in bronze welcoming his fans whenever they came to visit. It didn't seem real to me. Instinctively I wanted to give him a hug, but my height didn't allow it and so I contented myself with extending the arms to squeeze his leg. I held on with all my strenght, letting out a silent cry and hiding my face. The breath became more and more labored, but I quickly tried to calm down and enjoy that magical moment to pay homage to Freddie with a bouquet of flowers. I placed myself in front of him as if to capture that gaze which was majestically turned towards the horizon, where the deep blue of the water and the very high mountains seemed to be one. I admired him for a few minutes in disbelief and happiness, and it was as if there was no one around us. Me, him and the immensity of the lake.

I would have liked to stay in his company all the time, just *you and me*, but the comings and goings of people who incessantly photographed themselves, increased more and more, so I left, promising him that I would return the same evening.

It was the turn to visit the Mountain Studios, which were located nearby inside the Barriere Casino. What aroused my most interest was exploring what fascinated me, getting curious to know more, see and touch everything related to the band up close. All of this encouraged me to learn something new about Queen's life and career.

"*Queen The Studio Experience*" was written in black and gold, with a microphone drawn inside the Q. Being there, knowing I was stepping on the ground where Freddie and the other members of the band had walked, it seemed to me a dream coming true. At the entrance, to my right, the dedications dominated. I found a small space to stick a red heart and a montage of a photo of me with Freddie. Before arriving at the control room, I found myself into a totally Queen-branded environment. I lingered over Freddie's notes on scraps of paper, the stage costumes, photographs, musical instruments, various albums in the background. I put my hand on it. The glass partition was so thin that I felt like I was touching every written word. I've never been so close to him. Here emotion took over. I entered the control room. Knowing that I was in the same place where Freddie had been for so many years, where he spent the last days of his life and where the band recorded so many albums such as *Innuendo, Jazz, Made In Heaven* and others, it caused me an indescribable emotion, which hit me from head to toe, to then stop at my heart. On the monitor I saw Brian who through a video message, obviously in his language, said:

"*Hello! I'm Brian May. I hope you enjoyed visiting* Queen The Studio Experience *exhibition. Now I will tell you about* Mother Love. *This is the last song we recorded with Freddie. Imagine yourself here in 1991, sitting in the seat of sound engineer and producer David Richards. I was sitting to your left, busy writing the lyrics while Freddie was there sipping vodka and doing his vocals, when suddenly he exclaimed, "Write me more words." I gave him the lyrics and he started to sing, but we couldn't finish it and Freddie said:"I can't do it, I have to go and rest, then I'll come back and finish it". Unfortunately he never came back." Listening to Mother Love right there was a harrowing experience.*

I long for peace before I die
All I want is to know that you're there
You're gonna give me all that sweet mother love

These are the last lines sung by Freddie Mercury. Then came Brian's voice, which beautifully brought the song to a close. Finally you could hear the sound of the sea, the chirping of seagulls and the cry of a child. The cirle of life that closes. Back in the womb where you were safe and secure.

I felt the pain like a punch in the stomach. Where Queen had recorded seven albums, I could barely move a command to be able to remix, the emotion was so strong. On tiptoe I stopped at the point where there is a brass plate indicating the exact spot where Freddie recorded his last vocal parts, that May 13, 1991. I remained silent for a few minutes, respecting a life lived fully for himself and for us. I felt his pain. I clung to his courage and deep inside I thanked him for the heritage of humanity he had left us.

It was cold outside and the scenery was breathtaking. I was wrapped in a sense of peace and serenity, and the bodily sensation that led that moment, make me feel the same that Freddie found in Montreux in the last years of his life. I couldn't have asked for a better 50th birthday party. He was my most precious gift. At the restaurant I found many hearts hanging framed, and one in particular, quite large, surrounded by shrubs with red berries next to my table, which added to the 437 numbers of hearts found everywhere and which for me meant the presence of angels. My heart was full of him and happiness pervaded my whole body. I toasted to one more year of my life, but one more year with you, Freddie, was what got me above the clouds and it was wonderful.

As promised, in the middle of the night I returned to the lake for our *rendez-vous*. Standing next to his feet and looking at his fist to the moon, I felt small in front of him. As a non-smoker, I lit a cigarette anyway, to keep him company. It was dark and the lights of the *promenade* reflected on Leman making the atmosphere exceptional, and with Freddie next to me, even more sublime. I remained silent until the last pitch, as if to contain the thoughts that went through my head. I got up to seek his eyes and make him a confession:

"Freddie! Coming into my life has been one of the greatest gifts you have given me. You enhance the light and highlight the colors of the world around me. Thanks to you, now I also have many friends. Thank you for existing". My eyes inevitably went down to *Lover of life - Singer of songs* tab. "You knew loneliness well, because affection and friendship were not proportional to the number of people you were surrounded by, but I was making a virtue of this lack of you."

The dew had just begun to cover his shoulders, sliding down like a path just like his dripping sweat at concerts, after giving his peak performance. I got up to leave, carrying a little of that "sweat" on my hands, the result of so much pleasant live effort, saying "Goodnight, My Bijou" and giving him a kiss. I set off with the air in my lungs full of him, because the next day another adventure awaited me to discover, the Duck House.

The adrenaline was at very high levels and I could not sleep easily. I had yet to make contact with reality and realize that it was all true. You realize when you look closely, when you manage to leave a dedication, when you shiver, when you cry, when you see everything through his eyes and touch through his hands. I feel you never left Montreux. You are in the scent of the flowers that frame the lake, in the bench with your face, in your beautiful penthouse on the Quai des Fleurs, in your suite at the Le Montreux Palace Hotel, in every greeting that fans leave at the old entrance to the Studios, you are inside that fist to the sky, you are everywhere, you are on top of the mountains where only number ones can stand and you are free in those calm waters, I am sure you are there waiting for us all the time.

But above all, Freddie, you are in that lake house, where you were able to live in peace before and after in your last years, and which was the backdrop for your brilliant musical creativity.

The next day I decided to go on foot, to take a closer look at everything your eyes had seen every time you walked that road full of trees and Belle Epoque-style houses. I walked towards Clarens in the impatience of finding it, I quickened my steps with my heart that seemed to leave my chest, my breathing was more labored and the emotion of a teenager on a first date holding another sticker red heart.

House number 165. I stopped trembling.

The Duck House had a fairly low wooden door, from which part of the garden could be seen. I touched it everywhere I thought you had touched, and on tiptoe I leaned out to have a better look at the stairs that led down, and the grass that covered the ground everywhere. The secular trees gave an extra touch to that environment still left in the 70s. I stood there on tiptoe for a while, with my gaze peering at every possible and imaginable corner. I smiled at the thought of how nice it would be to see you, laughing and joking with Roger, John and Brian. Laterally there was a low wall from which the wooden house by the lake stood out, the background of the album *Made In Heaven*. I leaned over with my whole body despite the difficulty, in seeing what was beyond, and decided to sit near the corner where I could see it best. I imagined you there, sitting on a rocking chair, facing the bright red sky, with a pencil and paper in your hand, jotting down your thoughts letting yourself be inspired by the fabulous nature of Montreux, listening to the screech of the seagulls and occasionally giving a look at the swans quacking in front of you undisturbed. I wanted to stay there, in the doorway listening to your music for hours and hours, because I've never felt you so close. That feeling of well-being caused me joy. I don't remember how long I sat, observing the whole environment with joy.

When I got back, I put *A Winter's Tale* loud. Brian's guitar sounded like it was crying and screaming at the same time. I heard anger in your voice when you say *"Mountains are zooming higher"*, and felt a little resentment, because your're gone, you left us, and I only wanted to see you once live. It is difficult to resign ourselves to the loss of a person when they are constantly present in our lives. I promised I would come back and I keep my word…

Montreux has become synonymous with Queen and especially with Freddie. Ever the singer Lucio Dalla went to greet him, until one day fate united them forever, right there.

In the old studio there was a bustle of people who left their thoughts on the walls for this journey of passion dedicated to their idols. It would have been great if before leaving I could have met someone who had lived with Freddie…Peter or Jim Beach…Someone happened to see them and exchange a few words with. I wasn't that lucky, so I had one more reason to come back.

There is a first time for everything. A first time to go to school, to fall in love, to graduate, to take a plane, to get married, to have a child. Here, Montreux enters those important and unforgettable first times and will always remain in the heart of anyone who goes to visit Freddie and Queen, one of those first time that leave you with serenity and a great, huge desire to return and find other shades of the sky that his fist magically fades into different colors: pink, purple and orange, fiery red, the sand color of the desert and the yellow he liked so much.

It was just like Freddie said: *"Si tu veux que ton ame trouve la paix, viens à Montreux"*. *"If you want your soul to find peace, come to Montreux"*. *"Se vuoi che la tua anima trovi la pace, vieni a Montreux"*.

In whatever language he said it, the content has not changed even after thirty years.

***

"We have visited Montreux twice, it stays in your heart, as our beloved Freddie said."

"I too felt a great emotion, I cried, and I didn't want to leave anymore."

"I've been there twice, the first time in '97 there were still all the writings with the dedications, and I also put mine. I went back there in 2010 and that's it. Always exciting anyway."

"Before arriving I felt so excited, like I should go there and meet him. I'm sorry he left when I was just 4 years old. I think about it often. Because the joy and strenght that he gives me despite everything is infinite. I shared the song Bohemian Rhapsody with others who were there for the same reason. The least I could do to thank him. And in his garden two squirrels climbed up a tree and chased each other. I felt his presence and it was truly a unique emotion. Thank you Freddie!"

"I've been to Montreux twice and this year I'm going back with a friend of mine. It's a great place, as Freddie said. I felt his presence everywhere, also thanks to the people of Montreux who respect him very much! The

Studios then...a museum! It almost seems that his aura is there, waiting for visitors! Go there, spend some time with Freddie and you'll understand!"

"We often talk about Montreux, about the emotion one feels in front of that statue of Freddie in front of the lake, my heart was pounding when I saw it! And let's also talk about the atmosphere you feel when you enter the Studios, when you are in front of those costumes, those messy erased written sheets, all those things that are there and you know it's them but above all his! When you put on headphones and hear the story, the music and even if you know it well, it seems different there, more powerful, and you have the impression that he is there behind you."

***

There's a kind of magic in the air
A Winter's Tale (Queen, 1995)

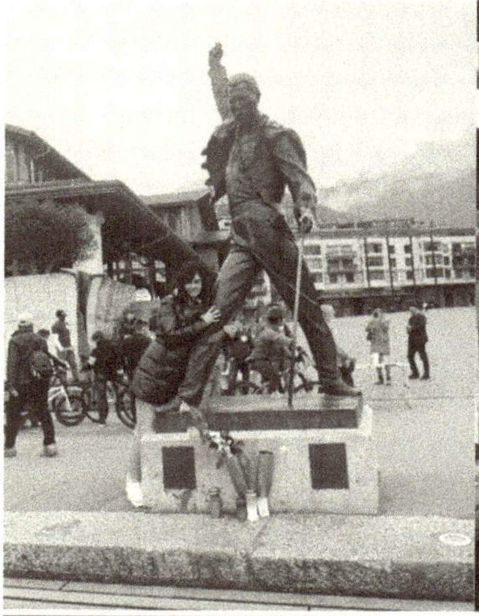
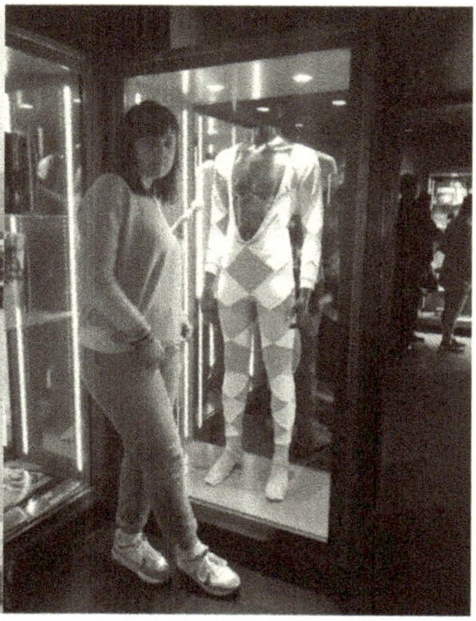
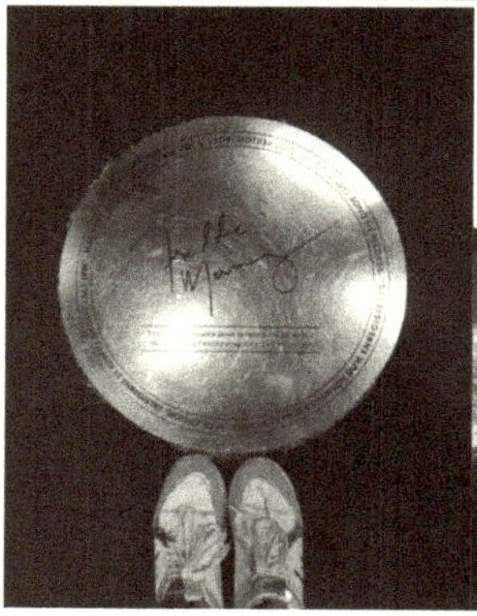
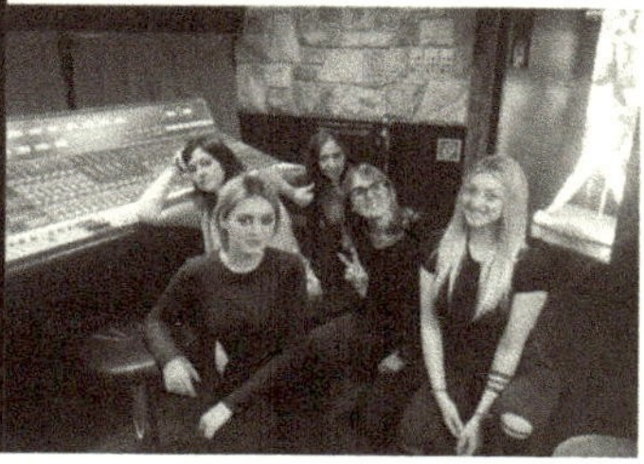
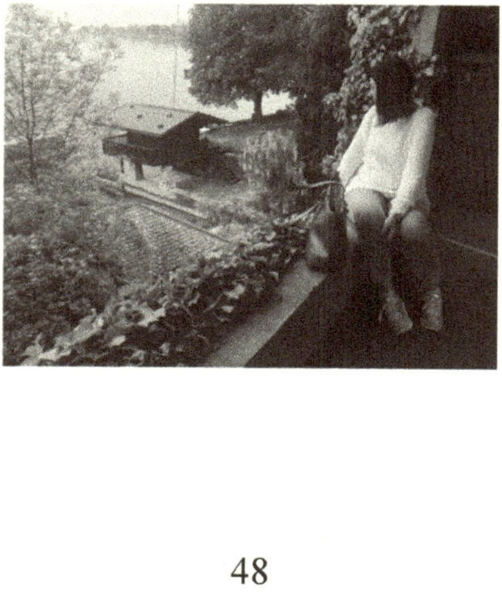

STYLE AND ELEGANCE

"I dress to impress but with a certain taste and I have fun with my stage clothes."
Freddie Mercury – Words and thoughts

Looking at photos of Freddie as a child, I noticed that from an early age he had a slim and agile physique which made him more suited to playing his favorite sports such as sprinting, table tennis, becoming champion in this discipline, but also hockey and boxing in which he was really excellent. When he grew up he managed to maintain this physicality which allowed him to get on stage to small contortion performances, full of eroticism and sensuality. When I walked up to the window for the first time at Mountain Studios in Montreux to get a better look at the orange, green and white argyle suit worn at Live at Earls Court '77, I realized that Freddie wasn't quite as tall as he looked on stage. His height wasn't measured in inches, but was associated with the stature of the leader he was.

The thin waist showed his thinness in the 70s, but despite this, he had a perfect physique. His long legs fit perfectly those overalls which, in its twists, made him unique and inimitable. His slender and graceful body, his agility and his constitution, made him energetic to such an extent that he could overwhelm anyone around him, with inevitable effects. His physique and the fact that he was very photogenic, allowed him at a very young age, to pose as a model at Ealing Art College in London, and later also to do a photo shoot for Vogue, for the promotion of men's diamonds. In a certain sense Freddie "promoted" himself, an authentic rare diamond. I stopped at another window displaying the ivory silk cape shirt, with the embroidered bodice with giant accordion pleats, that Freddie wore at the Rainbow Theater in '74, my favorite live. It was as if I had him in front of me as he spread his arms, and the width of the long sleeves made him look like a white eagle in flight. His explicit coquetry made him irresistible to the point of unleashing the greatest passions with devastating results, and the best example in us fans of Queen.

His lips are a reference to eroticism and his teeth become beautiful in the eyes of those who adore him, turning a defect into an asset. With the irony that characterized him he said: *"And then I don't like my protruding teeth. Sooner or later I'll have them fixed, but I just haven't had the time so far. Other than that, I'm perfect"*. How to blame him? His fine and straight nose like Michelangelo's David, together with his dark colors, made him perfection personified. His ebony black eyes, with a penetrating gaze, still reach straight to the heart, they fascinate you and enrapture your soul. His long fingers enchanted the audience as they glided over the piano keyboard, in such a delicate way that it conquered anyone. On stage, he fascinated me with his kimonos and diamond-patterned overalls, his glamour, black nail polish on one hand and demi-pointes. His style was so personal that it captured the attention of the public. I adored him in those photos with the Japanese kimonos that flattered him so much, and the sequined bodycon suits enhanced the character he had created. The looks that best suited his image were created by stylist Zandra Rhodes. But before her, Freddie himself drew sketches of clothes and also created a line, demonstrating a multilateral creativity.

His appropriate movements on the stage, his contortions and gestures, his make-up made the concerts into real theatrical performances. I found his particular movements inimitable, and he was unique and sensual in the way he handled that half-mast micropone which simbolically became a guitar, a baseball or golf bat, a rifle with an aiming like only Freddie could do or simply give a kiss to the man who accompanied him in his concerts, and who in the most emotional moments was the only one he could hold tightly.

And as he said: *"If you want to do something, do it with style."*

I was specifically struck by the vast choice and the particularity of the clothing he wore in the 70s. He was himself and went against the tide with his extravagant way of dressing at the beginning of his career, wearing jackets with floral fabrics, which he bought exclusively from Biba, and Indian brand. In his wardrobe there was no shortage of satin dresses, tight trousers, shoes with a little heel and very colorful long cardigans. On the other hand, in those years fashion imposed it like so many silver accessories, but what amazed me the most was his way of wearing them with class and elegance. In any case, he was always careful to choose the right look.

Often among us fans we ask ourselves if we like more the 70s or 80s Freddie. The beauty of Freddie is that he is liked in all ways, glamorous, sporty, tight, casual, because his physique and his physiology allowed him to be up to any situation. My curiosity was fueled by numerous video clips starting from the beginning, in those years when daring in the way of dressing and behaving was not for everyone. I was enchanted the first time I saw Freddie in *Killer Queen,* with the brown fur coat, satin pants and ankle boots. Being known for his histrionics, he put all of himself into the show, becoming a stage animal in his most absurd looks but which made him improbable and princely; always candid with white trousers and shoes, the color of the Zoroastrian religion, a sign of purity.

At the end of each concert he was always wrapped in various flags, a red fur cape and his triumphal king of rock crown, becoming the undisputed idol with his majesty. I was drawn to Freddie's command of the stage and his stage presence as a great entertainer of the crowd. And in the backstage my gaze inevitably fell on him, and when he looked at the camera he seeemed to return that gaze.

I like his transformation in the 80s, even if it was really radical. His distinctive face, short haircut, mustache made him more macho. The image most imprinted in the collective memory is that of Live Aid, where he magically kidnapped millions of people all over the world, given that the event went worldwide, broadcasting something special and beyond the schemes.

I also discovered that Freddie was a collector of ties, which he really like, even if he never wore them. His refined artistic taste fascinates me. And since his style was not manifested only in clothing and shows, he invested a lot in the purchase of Impressionist paintings, works by Victorian masters and Japanese woodcuts. He could often be seen consulting the catalogues. His house in London, Garden Lodge in the elegant district of Kensington, was furnished with fine antique furniture and objects, exclusively in the Chippendale style, complemented by paintings, expensive vases, crystals, antique carpets, works of art of value, which speaks volumes of the showman's refined tastes. I'm sorry I can't see up close these wonders that Freddie particularly cared about. One night I dreamed that I visited his house on a day open to the public, which rarely happened. I really hope that one day it can become a house-museum, so that we fans can also admire his personal tastes up close. In any case, each of us manages in his own way to describe the beauty and elegance that characterized him.

***

"Nature's brush has been generous with you. It designed perfect and decisive lines adding delicate and silky colors, with luminosity and shading, to underline and highlight the magical encounter between humanity and spirituality."

"The eighth wonder."

"As a popular Roman song says:"if a painter wanted to paint you, he would throw away his brushes and stay and look at you."

"His beauty is magnetic, you can't take your eyes off his face and body full of natural and spontaneous sensuality."

"Beauty that cannot be properly defined because it is so grand."

"He looks to me like a gentleman from the Italian Renaissance. One of the Medici family of Florence (in the photos from the 70s), while in the 80s he is more like Lawrence of Arabia. He has a delicate nose, but large, long (Middle Eastern) eyes and full lips. Big jaw typical of Persia and olive brown complexion. Black, curly, shiny hair (which he straightened)."

"That day, God or nature or the energy of the universe, whichever you prefer, put its hand to brushes and intense colors, and with a precise and decisive touch it traced perfect lines. Happy Sunday, bad guy."

"Good morning show of nature!"

"A masterpiece!"

"That day God was inspired."

"He made a man, not perfect, but his flaws made him special and gave him a wonderful voice."

"Masterpiece created with a precise purpose in mind. That purpose was fulfilled beyond all expectations, even of the creating artist who gave the challenge".

***

Yes, we were hungry, yes, we were brill (Ha, ha)
We were so dandy, we love you madly -
             Was It All Worth It? (Queen, 1989)

AN EMOTION INSIDE EVERY SONG

"During Love of My Life *I was overwhelmed by emotions, I swallowed with difficulty, I felt the same sensation that The Last Night of the Proms gives me. It was a wonderful audience and I liked their way of expressing emotions."*

Freddie Mercury – A life in his words

Music is the most powerful medium capable of causing multiple emotions, from pride to anger, from relaxation following a ballad to sadness, especially when it is associated with personal events. Most lead to joy, seduction, mirth and love. The energy that comes from listening to your favorite music, almost always turns into positivity.

Sometimes a song strikes you like a bolt from the blue and you can't explain it, as has also happened to other singers who love Freddie, for example Cesare Cremonini who proudly displays his tattoo, a sign of devotion to a hero, because he and his songs save us, as far as possible, from worries, loneliness, bad thoughts. I discovered that Freddie has become the idol of many other famous singers, such as Max Pezzali, Enrico Ruggeri, Robbie Williams, Lady Ga Ga, who was inspired for her stage name by the title of a song (Radio Ga Ga), and who knows how many others who will surely be inspired by him.

Over the years some of Queen's songs such as *We Are the Champions, The Show Must Go On, Radio Gaga, I Want To Break Free*, in short, the most broadcast ones, I had heard on the radio or seen on TV, but I didn't know anything else about their repertoire, much less Freddie's solo one, nor about his life, so I began to discover them a little at a time, savoring this discovery slowly as you do with a good wine, getting excited about each song which I heard for the first time. *Lily of the Valley,* this slow ballad softly sung by Freddie, became my lullaby during my sleepless nights. His intense voice enchanted me and entered me so much that I could not get out anymore. The songs that old fans had waited for, and heard over more than twenty years of Queen's career, I heard them in no time. Imagine the intensity of the impacrt of discovering them every day, one after the other. I found them unique in their genre: glam rock, hard rock, progressive rock, pop-soft rock, gospel, funk, heavy metal. A diversity of genres in which the interweaving and harmony of their voices created an unusual and particular choir, which inevitably became unmistakable for my hearing. Feeling them interwine with each other, just like the fusion of their eyes on the cover of *The Miracle*, I felt the amazement that comes when you feel overwhelmed by the manifestation of greatness. And when I closed my eyes for a moment, I allowed myself to sink into the sensation that accompanied that moment, finding the serenity that I had been missing for a long time, and that thanks to them I was finding again, but in the meantime Liar and Death On Two Legs, sung out loud, helped me to release anger for some events in my life, thus finding a balance that I had been looking for for years, never to go back, just like the title of one of their songs, *Nevermore*.

Unintentionally, as *Too Much Love Will Kill You* teaches us, we become *"victims of our own crime"*, because *"too much love can kill us"*, but listening to *Love of My Life* I physically felt how the expansion of the heart tried to valuing love, what heals you, encourages you, increases the entity of our dreams and our inner growth, makes you love yourself and strengthens the experience of this emotion.

It's a Hard Life, but I was able to deal with the strain of everyday life by listening to *Doing All Right and Don't Try So Hard*.

In *White Queen*, the piano solo stole my soul. While I still listened to it for hours and hours, each key of the piano became a letter of the alphabet, and overall they became words, sentences, tales of a keyboard that spoke, communicated, which amazed me and brought me up, making me soar above a stave without feeling the space between the lines. The wind of the notes and the key instead of the pilot made me touch the sky, feeling a pleasant sensation never experienced before.

For their lyrics Queen were often inspired by their personal life, relationships and events that happened, sometimes even historical ones, even religious figures. In general they varied, touching on different themes: love, friendship, loneliness, freedom, anger, nature, adventure. It was precisely in their verses that I found the teaching that encouraged me to face life. It was as if Freddie was advising me and at the same time addressing each of us.

Don't lose your head
Don't lose your way
Hear what I say
Don't Lose Your Head

Life is much too short to while away with tears
Jealousy

You've got a new goal
Headlong

If you fail, you mustn't grumble
Don't try so hard

That would really be a breakthru!
Breakthru

You just gotta be strong and believe in yourself
You start believing everything's gonna be alright
Make the bed light the light

Hammer to Fall

Just believe - just keep passing the open windows
Keep Passing the Open Windows

Keep yourself alive
Keep Yourself Alive

Just turn yourself into anything you think that you could ever be
Innuendo

    The coexistence of different styles, from progressive rock to operetta, passing through flamenco, and the significant video clip make this last song an excellent work. The personal teaching that I learned from *Bohemian Rhapsody* of the 90s, that is *Innuendo,* was the transformation that each of us should do to get to be what we want, abandoning the ego, destroying fear, removing the mask to move in total freedom.

    Seeing Freddie and Montserrat Caballé enter the stage hand in hand was a sparkling emotion to me, fueled by the flames coming from the brazier and the candles lit by the audience around them. The fire transmitted the warmth of a wonderful friendship. I found something unique in the union of pop music with opera, and in these two powerfully different voices. Freddie's versatile voice with its three and a half octaves, suitable for any musical genre, interwined in this duet with the two octaves of Montsy's (as he used to call her) soprano voice in Barcelona, exploded with all its force, thrilling me like never before. The words combined with the music became a hymn to true friendship. I can't help but quote Montserrat who later said: *"The difference among Freddie Mercury and other singers is that he had the voice".* I would add: "And not only that".

And when I came to hear the testament of Freddie and Queen, *Was It All Worth It,* with the summary of a career in a few simple and real words, I could not but reluctantly say that it was really worth it to have given us the soul, and for making us absorb your music with every pore of our body. I have listened attentively to your true testament, your story, Freddie; I let you tell me about it, being moved to hear you say that you were a happy man and that you loved us madly.

How I would like to listen to you, Freddie, but I can't hold back the tears that fall uncontrollably from the first notes of *The Show Must Go On.* Your voice to the nth power, the greatness of the lyrics and music accompanied by the images made from the best moments of your musical career, prevented me from holding them back. I let myself go into a liberating cry every time, because I realize once more that the show is not the same without you, because you were the engine that set it in motion, you were the fantasy, the true creativity, the perfection, you were the show within the show.

In *Made In Heaven,* however, his voice transported me to another dimension, high up in the white clouds I perceived emotions that were destined to be in heaven. Although a little late, Freddie called me into his kingdom and I was delighted to be a part of it. I was chosen, because thinking about it, not everyone who had seen the film had this effect.

My episodic memory was evoked by the slow rhythm but in the same intense way of *Mother Love,* which reminded me of critical events in my family, the end of a journey, nostalgia which in return makes me increase my positive attitude.

***

If I had to quote all the songs with the related emotions, and if I had to give a color to each emotion, I would create a rainbow with a thousand shades, capable of covering the sky and reflecting on the surface of the earth, bringing moods to float in the air, without feeling the force of gravity.

When people ask me "Don't you get bored listening to the same songs over and over again?", I reply "On the contrary. The more I listen to them, the more I want to listen to them again. Seeing is believing."

And that's right. I have heard their songs many times and the thousandth time I liked them just as wonderfully as the first time. If for fashion we say *haute couture*, for Queen's music we could say *houte musique*, or maybe it's better to use an absolute superlative? I didn't know exactly what the music of these four phenomena could be named, but I knew for sure that from then on there would be no other music for me. For Freddie's musical compositions, other axioms of communication should be added, such as *"You can't not sing it", "Content and emotions"* and *"Communication also takes place through contorsionism"*. Because when it comes to Queen, we fans are all a bit Watzlawick, a bit Haley and a bit Bateson.

Each song arouses in me an emotion linked to a fragment of my existence, even if strangely I hadn't listened to them in those precise moments of my life. Freddie sang romantic love, life, putting his heart and soul, often mentioning even the end of it, causing us fans an empathic pain, which we cannot accept, because some questions will never be answered, and what it would have been we can only imagine each one in his own way, but we will never be ready to give up the songs you would still have written and what you could still give, even if this readiness leaves room for gratitude for the immense treasure you left us together with the other Queen. When I was trying to figure out what you felt and wanted, I read and translated the verses. In there I found your world, your hopes, your prayers. It wa sas Freddie said: *"My life is in the songs".*

I realized that *I Was Born to Love You.* I was born to love you Mister Mercury, and everything I'm looking for in life, I find it in your music.

***

"There are emotions so deep and mysterious that they cannot be said or explained. You enclose them all, you reach the depths of the soul, you touch the heart with your caressing, strong, crystalline, persuasive voice. You've walked through life with all your vitality, you've searched for love, you've reached the top. You are Freddie, just you. My Fairy King *is just one of these songs. I listen to it often lately, and every time it surprises me both for the text that highlights Freddie's fervid immagination and for how it is musically constructed. Every time I imagine Freddie's hands shaking quickly on the piano, which is a protagonist instrument in this song. A magical world, fairy king. Who knows Freddie, maybe when you left 28 years ago, you flew right into that fairy world, into Rhye's Kingdom and are its king.*

"He taught me to laugh and cry. No shame in showing our emotions, I cried at several points, again. Love everyone for who and what they are."

"It all happens exactly to me too. At first I thought I was exaggerating but I read that I'm not the only one. Freddie takes the heart and soul and invades the mind. It's magic!"

"You are like a friend to us. A distant love. You are a world within us, a world of emotions and sensations that would never have been born if we hadn't met you. Still love you, Freddie."

"If there is a photo, memory or song that brings back a time of happiness for an individual, how can that be anything other than miraculous?".

"I'm just saying that the emotions I feel when I listen to Freddie are indescribable. I can go so far as to cry with emotion or to sing out loud laughing. He's unique. It's a mix of emotions that explode inside you, it's magical. I love him to death. He is my strenght. He is my life."

"And what I feel is quite easy to summarize, because when I listen to Queen I always feel only positive emotions. Curiosity, attention, but also lightness, amazement, fun, the desire to laugh and joke. Only sometimes, rarely, do I get a little melancholy thinking about the ungrateful and premature end he met. But I want to believe and hope that all the fan love still comes through. It must be so!"

"My darling, your songs are a total emotional upheaval. I hear and hear them endlessly, but every time I get excited as if it were the first time. And only you are capable of this, believe me my love. You are unique. You are special. You are my love."

"Thank you, Freddie! You music, your wonderful voice, your extraordinary talent, your beautiful soul and your heart full of love take me elsewhere, to another dimension and another time, where I can dream and feel deep and unique emotions. Thank you for being here!"

***

The songs always leave their mark on the mind of those who have attended one of his concerts, they leave a tattoo on the skin, an indelible mark that you carry with you for life and every time you look at it, it revives that emotion. We other fans who haven't had this luck, can only close our eyes and imagine being there for a moment through the precious story of this fan, which describes in detail what she went through on that very important day.

"Already in love with Queen since 1974. At the time, very little was known about these foreign groups but

I had many rock records, then they arrived and I lost my compass, and when I learned that they were arriving in Italy I didn't miss the opportunity. I couldn't believe it, I had a friend who had seen them in Slovenia and I told myself I absolutely had to go. My husband satisfied me. On the morning of September 14th with our Delta we ventured together with a friend of ours who was playing in a group. We sang from Turin to Milan always music by Queen, many tapes recorded by me from the radio or by someone who had some records. Once we arrived we walked towards the stadium...I suffer a bit of claustrophobia and I assure you that when the crowd began to enter I saw delirium, and panic began to take possession of me. I took my husband by the hand and with my eyes closed a little we came over half from the stage. Then slowly the show began, the wheels of the Metropolis *scene began to turn, there was smoke and I was about to miss the air. Freddie was about to arrive and when he entered and said "Ciao Milano!" I cried like a fool. I had always listened to him and now I saw him with his other companions, John with his bass that didn't move much, shy but big, Roger that beat like hell, and Brian in that white costume wrapped in a long red band, tall, thin, curly and fantastic on guitar...but I've always adored Freddie with his oriental charm, long hair like all my friends from the 70s, not very handsome but so charming, his movements left me speechless, seeing him there, jumping tireless here and there. His powerful voice always heard on records, I assure you that my hearbeats were no longer the same. When Liar began, which was the song that introduced them to me, I screamed louder than the kids I had close to me, but I didn't care at all, they were Queen, my idols, and when Freddie looked at me, (he certainly didn't look at me) I greeted him sending him kisses, and my husband looked at me amazed. Then comes Dragon Attack and there, guys, I started jumping like crazy, you can't help but do it, then again It's a hard life, passionate about opera, I knew he would do it like a God, and so on until the end when BRP arrives jubilation, banging my head when the song restarts after the break, and the pyrotechnic finale that made me jump. Beautiful! It's the end of the show with Freddie with the Italian flag, cheers,* God Save the Queen, *my regret not having photos, because at the time they didn't let you in with cameras. The only memory is a shirt now with holes but kept and worn only on certain occasions. Now the memories fade a bit, but I always have Freddie in front of my eyes and especially in my heart like his companions. For me it's the best group I've ever heard. The only regret is not having photos of the event, but my concerts have always been dedicated to pure listening and vision, and those were different times."*

Like her, Andrea also lived this beautiful experience live. When I read his testimony on a social network, I couldn't help but contact him and ask if he could describe to me what he had seen and felt having been present at a Queen concert and what it was like to see Freddie up close, and he kindly let me postponed the experience of that special day.

"I remember that morning of November 14, 1984, there was a heat just like in the most stifling days of summer. My friend Tommaso and I had arranged to meet at Santa Maria Novella station in Florence, to take the train to Milan at around 9 o'clock. The train left on time and the journey was pleasant. Of course there was talk of the concert, the songs they would sing, what the stage would be like. Information regarding the event was scarce. There was no internet. Arrived in Milan around 12 am we get on the subway and then get off at Piazzale Lotto S. Siro stop. Leaving the station, we head towards the entrance gates of Palasport where there was already a good group of kids waiting for the opening, which (if I remember well)

took place between 6 and 7 pm. As the hours went by, the people crowded in front of the entrance increased and together with them the heat too. As soon as we got inside, the stage appeared to us. It was a wonderful vision: it was huge, with hundreds of spotlights and the Metropolis scene as a backdrop. We ran to the foot of the stage, in the fourth or fifth row, slightly to the right. All that remained now was to wait for the concert to begin. At about 9 pm the lights of the arena were dimmed. A roar enveloped us. Pushing and crushing from all sides. Machines' notes came out of the amplifiers. Smoke covered the stage and the gears of the scenography began to rotate. Suddenly all 4 appeared in the fog; I shiver as I write. Freddie of course with his arm raised, and off with Tear It Up. Brian was wild; lights at full power. There is no peace under the stage. Then comes Under Pressure. It's a riot. But after a few arpeggios the notes of Somebody to Love start, and it's chaos again. Killer Queen was followed by an ovation. Then all the others (you know the lineup very well), up to It's a Hard Life, heard live for the first time like all the other songs by The Works. Very funny Freddie with the big wig on his head. The classic acoustic moment is also beautiful: an opportunity for everyone to catch their breath. Let's start again with Stone Cold Crazy. *Dazzling flashes and bangs come to the stage.* Another One Bites the Dust, *up to the apotheosis of* Bohemian Rhapsody *and* Radio Ga Ga. *Again Brian seals shields for* Hammer to Fall. *We live a dream. Freddie enters with the white guitar and off with* Crazy Little Thing Called Love, *with the classic streched out ending where the audience goes wild. The turn of* We Will Rock You *arrives and a little sadness comes to my mind: the concert is almost over. The whole Palasport sings and claps at the guitar solo. The first notes on the piano and* We Are the Champions *begins. The audience choir accompanies the band throughout the song until the moving finale. All fantastic and indescribable in words. We are at the end. The group says goodbye greeting the fans to the tune of* God Save the Queen. *This is the somewhat faded memory of that day. Many years have passed, but when I think of those moments, the emotion and nostalgia resurface indelible.*

***

"Mine are commercial love songs and I like to put my emotional touch on them. I write songs like this because in the end what I feel strongly is love, it's emotion."
Freddie Mercury – A life in his words

Let's share these words of love
Las Palabras de Amor (Queen, 1982)

FREDDIE IS SUPPORT, HELP AND TEACHING

"I think our music is pure escapism, like going to a good movie. It's aimed at those who want to go in there, see the show, forget about their problems for a while and enjoy a couple of hours, that's all. Then when he comes out he finds his problems and comes back again for a new escape."

Freddie Mercury – A life in his words

Freddie was a mix of talent, irony, charisma, genius, generosity, cordiality, *savoir faire* and values which together became an explosion from which came that spark that make him (and still makes him) special for everyone. If you know him, it's impossible not to feel love and admiration. Thank you for existing and merci beaucoup for the help you give us every day with your will to live, which you transit to us not only through music, but also through your way of being, the way you approached college at such a tender age, your humour, your being so kind and caring to everyone, your desire to have fun and live life to the fullest, your love for animals, the care you had for your cats and koi carp, esteem for your true friends, respect for your parents, mon Jer, dad Bomi and your sister Kashira, protection and privacy for them and for yourself. I know that from behind some clouds you look at us, you observe us and you laugh a few times, because sometimes we joke too, commenting on your movements, your body, but what really matters is the fact that in some way you help us to face life. It may sounds exaggerated, but to throw down this doubt are the true facts, everyday experiences and testimonies.

Each of us has dark moments in life, but Freddie with his extrordinary voice eased my wounds, made me forget the past but not the people who had left me and who are now in heaven with him, he helped me process the separations, he increased my self esteem, he taught me to fight harder, but most importantly he led me to an inner state of elation and appreciation of myself and of loneliness, when usually it is fear that conditions this way of being.

When I immerse myself in Queen songs, I think of nothing, I seem to be in the middle of nature and walking aimlessly, free, carefree, towards a goal. Their music has a therapeutic effect on me. It gave me the tranquility I needed and the strenght to face my chaotic days, eliminating the stress of everyday life. At night, incredibly, only Freddie's voice calms me down from that monster (srl syndrome) that takes over my body.

Through the verses of his songs Freddie supports us and teaches us to accept ourselves, not to pity ourselves, to keep control of destiny and accept challenges.

It's strange to say, but Freddie helped me make the right decisions. When I fell in love with Queen it was a moment in which I had to make a love choice towards myself by cutting off a lasting relationship, and what he said to Mary, *"You believe in me and I in you"*, was spinning in my head like a refrain. This teaching helped me to work out a not indifferent and strangely painless detachment, because Freddie was there every moment I thought about it. There was in particular with the verses of *Too Much Love Will Kill You*, which helped me to make a decison.

Too much love will kill you if you can't make up your mind

But slowly I managed to face the situation with the right calm and I always have to thank Mr Mercury, always and only him.

Freddie taught us to trust ourselves. Even starting from nothing you can do so far, just have a goal in life, which must be fueled with talent, constant work and a lot of passion. And while he climbed the ladder to success he had fun, fell in love, suffered from lonelines, but he moved and positively influenced generations of fans.

For me Freddie is an open book, but for many other people he seems to have pages to decipher, because basically his mystical appearance was nothing more than a protection towards himself and his loved ones. For fans it is the easiest alphabet to read and understand to the point of drawing lessons from its demonstrations. We know that language as easy for us as it is difficult for journalists and the press. He was a humble and selfless person who helped others and people in need without wanting to appear in the tabloids, as in the case of the donations he made for AIDS research, and beyond. He also often helped people in need, even though he didn't know them.

***

Freddie had a very clear vision of his role as an artist. This awareness of his, teaches us to think and understand who we really want to be, what we want to do in life and how to try and obtain it, and that we can achieve the chosen goals while always remaining humble and polite. I find really intelligent his way of dealing with situations with charisma and irony, a behavior to which one cannot fail to refer in accepting events with serenity, even the most unexpected ones that life throws before you, the changes that derive from them, without backing down, rather giving yourself to others until the end. And it is precisely through the true testimonies of his fans that we understand more how much Freddie helps and supports us every day. Here are some.

"Your disarming charm. Your genius out of the ordinary. A strength so gentle, a sweetness so impetuous. Silence, peace, passion, fire. All together, harmoniously mixed in one person. Would you have ever tought, Mr Mercury, that your music, your choices, your smile would have helped so many people? You must be proud of it,

wherever you are, because in your simple inventiveness there is an unstoppable force. You made it. I still love you."

"It is true. Anyone who doesn't love him will think we're crazy. Yet Freddie. I'm talking about myself, but there are many of us, he helped me and still does with his wonderful voice, with his courage, with the will to live that he had until the end. He liked to give gifts to see people happy. My love, you make me happy. You are with me in every moment of my day, of my life. I hope you get the love we feel for you, I hope so, and you laugh at my jokes about you, but yes, you will laugh with that sweetest smile and you will be there until my last breath. I love you. Thanks."

"After a very busy day, I come home, turn on your music at full volume and finally empty my mind of all negative thoughts. I look at this photo, and I can dream of being elsewhere, in another time and place, where there is grace and beauty and passion. So, his songs, his voice, his presence in my life, just saved me."

"When I struggle to live and against difficulties I think of him, of his courage in facing the disease and he is an example for me, I bring out my strenght, as he taught us, and I face everything, I listen to his music and I cheer up, I change my mood becoming positive. Freddie is here with us."

"He helped me overcome a thousand adversities, most recently a bad illness and my father's death. And ten year ago also my mother's. Anyone who finds this ridiculous is soulless! Thank you love of my life."

"Hello! Sadly I lost my partner about two years ago. He was my whole family. I have no relatives or children, so he was my life, when he died the world collapsed on me and the atrocious pain was destroying me in the worst way. I didn't want to live anymore and I was about to give up, when Bijou turned on the radio and that line, "You And Me", gave me a small glimmer of hope, and here I am. It's not ridiculous, believe me, and whoever

finds it ridiculous means that il lacks human warmth. Freddie I love you! Thank you for having been in my live for thirty-one years. Thank you. My Bijou."

"Queen's music and Freddie's charismatic and positive presence help me every day. I listen to them in the morning, during the bus ride (which would seem endless without them) and then in the evening when I get home, it's a wonderful feeling to let myself be cradled and let the stress of the day slip away. Believe me when i say «Oh, thank goodness, I'm putting the music on now»."

"Freddie was the salvation of my life in a dark period, even if unfortunately he is no longer there, I will be eternally grateful to him, and I like him so much."

"In the sad and dark moments that I went through, it was enough for me to listen to him to feel better, to relieve my moods, and I was fine, he gave me so much strenght to go on, it moves me, I cry about it but it serves to facing what perhaps I would never have been able to overcome on my own."

"My support, thanks Freddie".

***

When your problems seem like mountains
Feel the need to find some answers
You can leave it for another day
Don't Try So Hard
Don't Try So Hard (Queen, February 4, 1991)

FREDDIE BECOMES PASSION

"Over time, if you have maintained success, you also have a following of people who have grown up with you. They continue to follow you and accept whatever you do: this is a devoted and passionate fan in my opinion. A fan who believes in what you do."

Freddie Mercury – A life in his words

Passion is such a strong feeling that it dominates a person, which makes it no longer a pastime, but a useful and precious time that is pleasantly filled. When Jimi Hendrix became Freddie's idol, he covered the walls of his room with his posters and went to see him in concert.

"Jimi Hendrix is very important. It's my idol. Somehow he summed up, with his live performance, all aspects of the work of a rock star. You can't compare to anyone. Either you have magic or you don't. No one can take his place."

I could very well appropriate these words from Freddie, because that's exactly what I would say about him. Freddie started dressing like Jimi and taking pictures just like him. In one of them, he plays the guitar on top of a colorful carpet. He also made drawings of himself. Sometimes I too try my hand at very simple drawings, which however give me great satisfaction. He had a passion for Hendrix, as I have a passion for him, and this is a particularly strong feeling, which arouses instincts of strong attraction and serves as a motivation for continuous dedication. The cause that unleashed this passion, was the very strong attraction I felt towards him, but in the passion that should dominate my mind I managed to find a balance between emotion and reason. When you idealize a person you like so much, weaknesses become strengths, flaws become strenghts, vices become virtues and trying to look like him or dress like him, or with the same colors, is part of the feeling you have in his comparisons.

Brian says the emotion he felt for Jimi Hendrix led him to think anything was possible. For this very reason I was fascinated by his perseverance, and his determination to get to do what he thought he did best, sing and entertain. This fostered a very keen interest and a loving transport in Freddie. The passion for Freddie also arose from the fact that he became the best frontman of all time, and after his death also a legend, just as he wished, and his way of doing as an artist along with his work since perfectionist were an example for me to follow.

His grit and strenght entered every part of my body. The curiosity to know more increased, making me spend hours and hours learning more about him. I went into the details of his life, from birth to the end of his days. I learned that he was born in Zanzibar on September 5, 1946, and everyone knows this, but I wanted to add something more for those who are not fans. It was a Thursday at 5:10 in the morning, just Parsi New Year's Day, precisely in the main public hospital, called Mnazi Mmnoia, located by the sea in the outer part of Stone Town (at the intersection of Kenyatta Road and Gizenga Street), one of the most important cities of the island, and was registered at the registry office 15 days later, exactly on 20 September, with the name Farrokh Bulsara. His surname originates from the Indian tourist city Bulsar (now Valsad) in southern Gujarat, where the family came from.

I was happy to know he had spent a happy childhood with his parents, his father Bomi, his mother Jen and his little sister Kashmira, until at the age of 8 he moved to Panchgani, near Bombay (since 1995 Mumbai), in India, where he attended St. Peter's School. Despite everything, little Freddie was attentive to his parents, and I discovered this through the letters he sent from time to time, recounting what happened to him, expressing his concerns as in the case of his sister Kashmira's health, but also his happiness as in the case of winning the Best All Rounded Junior trophy, and in learning piano lessons with Mrs. Smith. In the future, I would like to go to Zanzibar to see up close his home, his neighborhood, his world when he was little, and the Seven Seas of Rhye, his imaginary sea, but also the real one, where he went every day after drank his orange juice.

  I had entered the vortex of Queenmania, or rather of Freddiemania, but at that moment in my life they were the light at the end of the tunnel, lighting my way. I bought all the CDs and live DVDs of this legendary group and also the solo ones of "Queen". Thus it was that Freddie became everything to me: a friend, a brother, one of the house, the one who speaks to me and comforts me through the verses of his songs.

  In one verse of *Don't try So Hard,* Freddie sings: *Thank you lucky star*. Freddie, my lucky star is you. Your photos, books, CD and DVD collections, gadgets, your favorite bars of soap, drinks, candies, even your cigarettes. You fill me with your presence and that makes me feel good. Buying the perfumes you used is like feeling on your skin, and tasting your favorite chocolates, making a toast with vodka and Schweppes tonic or drinking your favorite tea, is like being in your company for a while.

  When I listened to *The Invisible Man* for the first time, although the title didn't refer to you, I thought "Now you are more visible than ever", and Taylor's voice reinforces the concept, when at the 19th second strongly calls you *"Freddie Mercury"*, just like any fan would like to call upon you. When I don't listen to you for a while I really go through withdrawal, but when I put my headphones on loud, it seems to me that you are in my room, in my life and in my head…and everywhere.

  You are there when I get up in the morning, and I travel to work, and I sing with you, and it seems to me that

I am not out of tune, you are there when I work because I play your wonderful songs to the children, and they clap their hands and feet at the rhythm of *We Will Rock You*, even if they can't coordinate their movements because they're too small, you're there when I get home and while I'm doing my chores, the broom stick becomes a microphone and I feel like making your moves, you're in the smile of my daughters Samantha and Letizia when I sing *I Want To Break Free*, despite the noise of the vacuum cleaner, you are there when I get ready to go out and I turn towards your photo with your gaze following me wherever I move, asking you if I look good dressed like this, you are among those many hearts that I have found in the last three years…you are alive…you are life…you are my queen of hearts.

"Enraptured in the mirror of your eyes, I breathe your breath. And I live". This is the sentence from the chocolate I unwrapped thinking of dedicating it to you, and a more beautiful sentence could not have happened, because your eyes are an open book for those who want to read them, your eyes tell an extraordinary life, your sufferings, your joys, your music. When I look at the photos it is as if I immediately understood if you were happy, sad or thoughtful at that moment. Well, I didn't choose you. *Maktub*. The destiny I believe in so much, has put you in front of me. You allow me to escape from the pain and find confirmation in your verses and many in your beautiful smile. I am proud to be your fan and I will never stop thanking you for all that positive energy you give me.

You said you didn't want to change the world and that you left your songs to express sensations and feelings, and you managed to get thousands of people in your grip, to make them sing and move like no one had ever done. I am reminded of *Radio Ga Ga*, at Live Aid, where hands clap in unison and nobody is out of time. And miraculously miraculous, they obediently perform your *"Eeeeooo"* in different versions, all taken by the current of energy that you emanated. You were incredible but it was all so real that it was impossible not to interact.

***

Freddie was an exceptional person, kind and polite to everyone, a very talented artist, and it was inevitable to be struck by his person and character, by his theatricality and his unique voice. If you really know him, it's impossible not to be influenced by him. I was struck by the comment of a fan, in those words I find myself completely.

"I love someone I've never seen and I miss someone I've never met."

Briefly, other fans describe him like this:

"Freddie is a character that everyone should know, especially kids who need ideals to take flight. But everyone can benefit from his example. The strength of dreams, the stubbornness in making them come true, love, the freedom to be yourself, respect for the family who did not share his style entirely, love for one's work, the strength of life against disease, acceptance of one's destiny. And of course the unique talent and genius, in his case in the field of music. Freddie was all of that. And all of this is for all of us. I don't think he was created to age, I know it's bad to say. But it had to be an immense firework, marvellous, which pierces the sky, which does not last long but that little is forever, for those who observe it."

"Freddie takes to the heart, to the brain, like a tender lover, he develops in a constant, intense way within us. His beauty is not only external, it is the fire that flares up inside, it is that joy that explodes like never before, it is pure passion."

"It is the call of kindred souls, something divine that is difficult to explain even to ourselves. His beauty is pure, it's in his eyes, in that spark that always bruns and

reminds us that every moment is worth living, with that passion that makes everything wonderful. His soul shines in us, and ours nourishes him and makes him live forever. His beauty is in his gestures, in the grace of his profound being, which is reflected in that so energetic and beautiful figure that we know but who has so much to give and say, offering us a depth, his own, rich in every feeling positive. A clean soul that makes him the most beautiful creature in the world."

"*Freddie is um Ser Humano Iluminado, belíssimo por dentro e por fora, que mantém todos unidos, porque a Sua áurea é autêntica e verdadeira, é puro amor o que Nós sentimos por Ele e vai ser assim sempre e para sempre*".
"*Freddie is an enlightened human being, beautiful inside and out, who holds everyone together, because his aura is authentic and true, what we feel for him is pure love and always it will be.*"

"*Freddie had a perfect connection with his fans.*"
***

Shared passion is a multiplied passion. Precisely for this reason, I created a small group called *We Are The Champions*. Sharing is like opening a window to the world from which enthusiasm, smiles, joy come and go and where this gesture becomes essential. The miraculous power of sharing means that the exchange of ideas, enrichment, news and plans for future trips increase the curiosity to know more and more.

Sonia is among those fans who are part of the smaller group and wanted to name her story. She lives in Turin and is a few years younger than me. There was an understanding with her right away. A few public comments and later in private, where we found ourselves both in character and in the way we approached Queen, but above all Freddie. When she sent me a photo of her from many years ago in London, I told her that she looked identical to a friend of mine, and that once I met a person who looked a lot like her, a girl I had seen in 1991 when I was living in Lecce, and which I would have stopped if it hadn't been for my boyfriend who prevented me. I had arrived in Italy a few months ago, and the lack of lifelong friendship was so strong that I dared to stop a stranger. Surprisingly, Sonia told me that in those years she spent every summer in Lecce, because her parents are from there. I like to think that girl was her, because I am of the opinion that people who are destined to find each other sooner or later will make it. Like our similar story with Freddie. We found it after so many years, because it was written like this in our destiny.

When I asked Sonia how she had approached Queen and especially Freddie, she sent me a vowel. Unlike a written message, where the writing goes straight to the heart, in the vowels you also perceive that tone of the voice, the emphasis, the mood, you feel the breath changing during the story, you catch the emotion by listening carefully. In a calm voice she began to tell me:

"Basically yes, I've seen the film, and I've always liked him, the way you like a singer. I went to watch the film, and then I watch it and I watch it and I watch it again and I notice that there is something that attracts me but I don't know what. Then I let it go. During the first lockdown one day I woke up to a Freddie Mercury song, Love of My Life, and...I was listening to it and I really don't know how to describe it. The more I listened to it, the more I felt the shiver...I had to be part of that world. However, this person had to enter me and I into him. It's a very strange feeling. I hope you understand me. We had to belong together. We were supposed to be there every day. It was (there was a moment of silence) ... *like a drug. I began to have the need to hear and see it every day, because I have to hear and see it every day, and therefore, nothing. I started reading, doing...it was something exceptional* (her laugh was heard which seemed to be contented. *In a month*

and a half I got Freddie's first tattoo, and the more I went on, the more this thing grew. Many times I even got scared, because I said: Where is this thing going to take me? It took me to organize the trip to Montreux, while obviously everything was still closed due to the pandemic. I felt the need to go to Montreux. My partner follows me everywhere anyway, because he likes Freddie Mercury, not as exasperated as me. He has been listening to them since he was six years old. On 15th the borders with Switzerland opened, on 18th I was in Montreux, heheh (her voice expressed joy). *I cried inside the Studios, I didn't sleep for days either before or after. Nothing, this thing has brought me to a level of madness greater than what I can imagine, and today I can't help it...I'm completely addicted to it (laughs)...it's impressive...I repeat, I have to hear him every day and many times when I walk in the middle of the street (maybe I'm crazy, who knows), I feel that he is with me. I look at the windows and feel like smiling for two because he may like that dress too rather than...well, this is a bit me with my emotions. I thought no one could figure out why I'm a little out of line, so this is me."*

I replied: *"Dear Chipsina* (nickname I gave her)*, I totally understand you. I'm glad I found someone who also understands me."*

***

Francesco is another member of the group who lives in Valentano in the province of Viterbo. Later his wife Annarita and his son Gabriele (who plays Queen songs as a small fan) joined as well. Francesco was lucky twice by accident and tells his experiences like this:

"It was December 1996, three weeks after unveiling Freddie' statue. I went to the Mountain Studios and hearing music coming from inside. I rang the bell and, after my insistence, the door opened and I found myself in front of Jim Beach. I was excited. He told me it was not

possible to enter, so I insisted a lot, saying that I came from Italy on purpose, and I could not fail to see the Studios. So I moved him (yes, I know it shouldn't be done, but understand me) and went inside. I was able to see them as they really were for a few seconds before being rightly kicked out. A few days later I learned that Michael Jackson had also been there to rehearse. Instead a few years ago I went to London. I was at the door of Garden Lodge, and she passed me. As she walked, perhaps she turned to see if she had been recognized. Having seen a photo shortly before, I recognized her immediately. But I knew of her confidentiality and I didn't ask her anything. I followed her at arm's lenght for a block and then I remembered I had the...phone! So I started filming without disturbing and always keeping a distance until she got into a taxi.

Then he attached a video that he himself had put on the internet, where we saw a fan taken aback to see the great love of Freddie Mercury. Mary could be seen walking towards a taxi. You could hear the noise of the cars and Francesco's voice near the telephone which in the meantime was filming on his mobile. *"It's Mary, Mary"* he repeated incredulously, in a voice that kept fading from atonishment and that only he could hear. She got into the car she was waiting for and he, with the expression of someone who is surprised, repeated her name again, with the cadence of someone who is letting go of a unique opportunity, without asking her for an autograph or a photo out of respect. He had only admired her from a distance of a few meters, continuing to repeat *"Mary"*.

"I swear, my heart was racing" he adds feeling privileged. I think his heart was two thousand, or maybe hundred thousand a million. For us fans there is no measure that is enough to show how much an emotion is worth.

***

Ivan is 31 years old and the youngest of our group. He comes from the beautiful land of Sicily. I met him in a group through his painting but above all papier-màchè works, obviously largely dedicated to Queen and Freddie. He tells me his fan story:

"I discovered Freddie and obviously Queen when I was 4 or 5 years old, in an unusual place. I was hospitalized for an operation and after carrying me along a red corridor, one of the doctors turned on the radio which was broadcasting Radio Ga Ga, *and it was immediately love at first listening. My mother told me that whenever I listened to it, I clapped my hands and hummed the lines. Freddie was like a guardian angel. I was so small that over the years I didn't follow this band on my own, but as a teenager I rediscovered it. Thus was born subsequently the passion, both for me and for my brother, for painting and papier-màchè, and over the years our creations have decorated our home, especially with representations of Queen and Freddie, giving us great personal satisfaction. Nowadays my love for Freddie is more intense; no one else in the world can convey the same emotions to me."*

***

Giuseppe is 39 years old and is a musician. He sent me an audio saying strong words. *"I can honestly say that I speak from the heart: I don't listen to Queen, I live and breathe them and therefore I describe to you the sensations I felt and still feel today. I discovered Queen in 1993 when I was 11, thanks to a tape my dad had. Even today I can't explain how I literally got kidnapped by this group, at the time without understanding anything about music. I state that I grew up into a family of musicians who liked all the hard rock of the 70s. Queen have been my first form of identity, starting from that summer '93 with Greatest Hits 2, which I listened to non-stop. Even today I can't figure out what is the mystical factor that kidnapped me, but I know that Queen gave me an identity and I found a curious character in Freddie Mercury. From then on I started buying and looking impatiently, bearing in mind that these were different times when not everything was exposed on the internet like today, hungrily asking my older brothers if they had anything about Queen. Being madly enraptured by the character of Taylor, at the age of 15 I began to study drums, often watching the video cassette of Live at Wembley. Initially my bed and my pillow became a drum which with the help of two wooden spoons made its first sounds and I sang and I was Roger Taylor. I loved drawing so much and having attended art school, which I have in common with Freddie, I started drawing Queen from all sides. I discovered Queen in the 70s through music magazines. I remember the first time I heard* Bohemian Rhapsody, *I was completely hooked. Even today I can't explain how this type of "drug" has never bored me. I began to fall in love with vocal harmonies. I am overwhelmed by the courage and tenacity that a person must have in proposing a piece on the radio where there is opera inside rock, investing everything because he truly believed in it, putting his mark in a superb way, with his conviction and courage."*

***

This great passion has allowed me to discover people with whom has born a relationship that goes beyond being a fan. A true, deep, sharing friendship has been established, a bond that cannot be broken because Freddie, our idol, is the glue. And even if we no longer look forward to the release of a record, the next concert, or to see them in person, we do not miss the opportunity to meet and remember them anyway or to go see an exhibition with their original photos.

***

January 21, 2020

As soon as I learned of the exhibition in Bologna with the images of the band's official photographer Denis O'Regan, I didn't hesitate even for a second to decide to go and visit it. While stopping at one of the stations, I saw a train with Jazz written on it. Just like one of Queen albums. Instead, outside the train station, I found myself in front of a large Hotel called the Mercure. I smiled at these important clues, which told me why I was there. It was a cold winter morning, but that didn't stop me from walking through the beautiful historic area of the city to get to *One Arte*. On my way to the exhibition site, I found the Cartier shop, and a little further on, I saw the inscription *Mary Beauty* on a shop sign. It seemed to me the fairy tale of the Grimm brothers, when Hansel and Gretel marked the route with white pebbles to find their way. These words were showing me the way. I was almost there when I met up with three other fans, and together we reached this small studio, located downtown. There were few photos, some in black and white that portayed them during the concert of 21 June '86 in Manheim in Germany, and some shots came from the two historic evenings, among the most amazing concerts, in London at Wembley Stadium. It was exciting to put yourself in the shoes of the official photographer. He had been in front of Queen...

  O'Regan has taken photos on stage and backstage in every European city, and he is the author of the famous photos from an helicopter rended by Queen, as they reached the last concert of the Magic Tour. They seemed to have been taken on the day itself, current and beautiful in very large formats. I was happy to see them up close, personally signed by him. Outside, the dark winter afternoon highlighted the lights of the hanging words of various songs, that are spread over the streets of the center in Bologna. We could do this in any city, with significant verses from our Freddie.

***

*"You can be anything you want to be
just transform yourself into everything you think
You can be free in your movements, be free, be free."*
Innuendo (Queen, 1991)

Here are some creations that fans have dedicated to Freddie and Queen: painting, works with papier-màchè, crochet, handcrafted work with wood, book sculpture with the bookfolding technique, sculpture in white terracotta and also drawings, among such as that of Veronica, a 6-year-old girl..

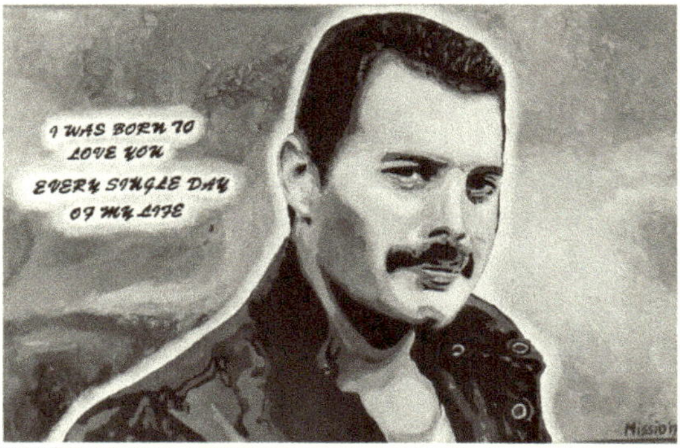
I WAS BORN TO
LOVE YOU
EVERY SINGLE DAY
OF MY LIFE
Mission

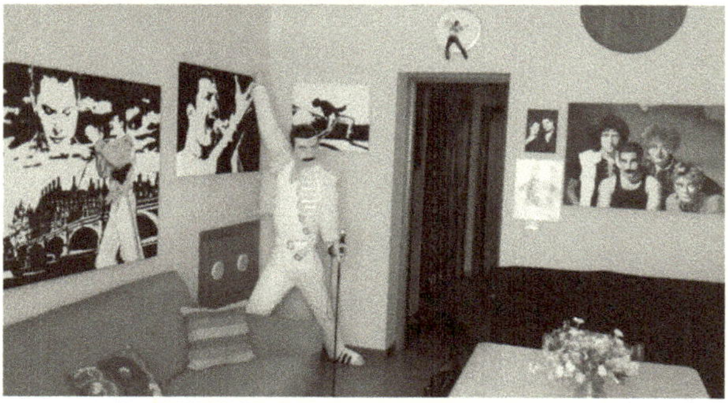

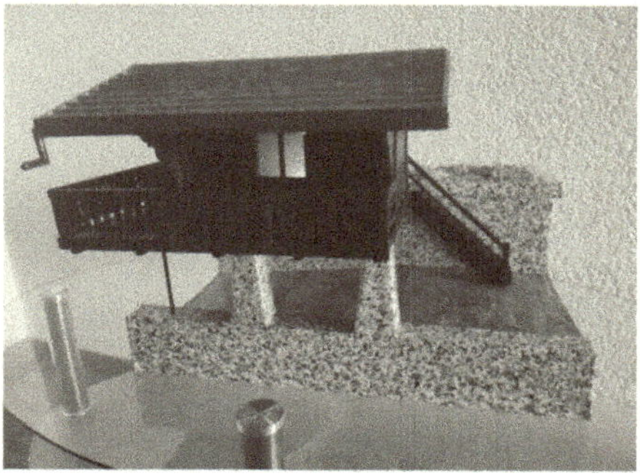

85

SOMETHING ABOUT ME

"I was a precocious child and my parents thought that boarding school would help me grow up. So when I was about seven years old, they picked me up in India and sent me for a while. It was an educational upheaval, which seems to have worked, I'd say."
Lesley-Ann Jones, *I Will Rock You*

Before continuing to describe (I hope to convey my emotions to you again), I wanted to tell you something about myself, based on these words from Freddie, *"I'm sure there are many people who see themselves in me"*, because I see myself in him on many things. I was born into a non-practicing Muslim family. The only thing that I carry with me from this religion, is a phrase that I heard from my mother before going to sleep: "*Bismillah Rahman e Rahim*", so much so that I use it too. I can't tell if it was a kind of prayer (it means 2 in the name of Allah") or a blessing. Surely it brought luck to Freddie, this key word of *Bohemian Rhapsody*. I know it's part of the Koran, even though Freddie was a Zoroastrian.

I was born in 1969. That same year, during a performance on 9 September at The Sink in Liverpool, the first meeting among Freddie, Roger Taylor and Brian May took place, and it is the year in which Freddie finished high school. After Ibex, Mercury joined Taylor and May into the Smile. And it was precisely that year that the British citizenship of the Bulsara family was registered.

Many years ago the Parsis fled to India from Persia to escape the persecution of the Muslims. Instead, in 1964 in Zanzibar there was a revolution against British domination, and the Bulsara family, like all other Indians, was forced to go and live in another country within six months. Freddie and his family moved to London when he was still Farrokh Bulsara. The origins of this name derive from the Persian, which means "happy, lucky", and his name day falls on November 1st. I thought that, for Freddie, changing his name didn't mean changing identity, but moving on.

I was born and raised in Albania, a country where the dictatorship reigned and it was forbidden to listen to and sing foreign music, even if many people did it secretely and I was one of them. I know it sounds absurd, but it was exactly like that. The total lack of freedom of speech, and the right to listen meant that people, mainly young ones, secretely listened to the songs of other nations (especially those in English, Italian and of neighboring countries, Yugoslav and Greek). I won't list the extreme consequences, but they weren't pleasant at all. But in any case, I was passionate about music, and I followed it as best as I could.

And it was precisely on one of those nights, I believe back in 1989, when I was up late stydying for university exams, and on a channel in the former Yugoslavia called *Shkup,* I saw the performance of a singer with mustache, dressed in jeans and a white tank top. This is the dèja-vu I was talking about in the first chapter, looking at the first images of the film, when Freddie prepares to enter the stage, and of course I had just learned the name of the event when I was watching the film. I immediately liked the fast and melodious rhythm of *Radio Ga Ga* song, but above all I was struck by this singer, who casually ran up and down the stage, from left to right and viceversa. I was used to seeing static singers, because the dictatorship also forbade dancing. I didn't quite understand who he was, because I had to turn off the TV when my mother entered the room. She didn't want me to watch concerts or video clips, for fear that the neighbors would overhear us: at the time the consequences included quite severe penalties, and therefore she kept repeating this to me constantly. I remember that in that period the police went around the houses to check the antennas, so that nobody had the possibility to follow the "models" of capitalism through television.

However, going back to that night in 1989, I didn't find out who that charismatic singer was, and for years I never had the opportunity to see him or listen to his songs, even though I often listened to the hit parade with my ears attached to the radio, since 1983. I remember many songs at the top, but strangely none that reminded me of Queen. Maybe, not knowing the Italian language, I often didn't understand who was singing them.

In March 1991 (the year Freddie died) I decided to leave my country in search of freedom, reclutantly leaving my career as a basketball player, and the last year of university, wich luckily I was able to recover after four years, managing to graduate in primary sciences. In the months before his death, Queen were not talked about so much, or at least I don't remember it, and in those days I had other things to think about, because life as an immigrant was not easy, thus putting hobbies, passion and pleasure in the background. I don't remember exactly the year, I think I had just been in Italy when MTV broadcast *Radio Ga Ga,* sung at Live Aid. Curiously, I approached the TV and instantly reconnected the image of the singer in light jeans and a white tank top that had stuck in my mind, waiting for the song to end in order to read the title and his name, but I didn't elaborate on who he really were. Queen and their singer and what career they had previously had, on the other hand the absence of the internet in those years, limited information a lot. During these years, few people have taken the train with me, but many of them have gradually got off at different stations. Unfortunately not all people are who we think they are, and after disappointments and broken promises I decided to close the doors of my heart, coincidentally in the same period in which I discovered Queen. In that moment of displeasure also for other personal events, it was Freddie who healed the wound: his gaze gave me strength, his voice calmed my soul and healed my heart.

I felt his presence around me, or so I wanted to believe. It was Queen with their timeless songs that made me think positive. And life went on along with a project about Freddie that I had started in February, and that kept me busy all summer, spending hours and hours on the computer well into the night. I was letting my creativity run wild without thinking about how it would turn out or if it would like it. Nine months of pure passion and dedication. And as with every birth, the greatest happiness comes when you hold your baby tightly in your hands: in my case, this work made up of 150 pages in PowerPoint in which, among photos and captions found in various books, Freddie tells fragments of his life, from when he was little until his last days.

Just on September 5, 2019 I went to pick it up at the typography, and it was my first gift for Freddie's birthday. I can't describe what I felt as I touched the glossy pages. The hand glided lightly and I thought I could hear his voice, as delicate when he spoke as powerful when he performed. A unique book of its kind that I keep with fanaticism at home, in the space I have dedicated to him. Here, this is the story of a special encounter, of an inner transformation, of a favor that was done to me in being preferred, I believe by a force majeure, because what I am feeling is something extraordinary, and even though I know that I won't be understood by everyone, the important thing is to experience these beautiful sensations that keep me alive.

***

I want to make you a supersonic
Don't stop me, don't stop me
Don't stop me now (Queen, 1979)

AFFINITIES AND COINCIDENCES

"I was born in Zanzibar, which was then part of the Commonwealth...Growing up in India I saw a lot of poverty. It's usual when you live there. I belonged to the middle class, but I think I always gave the impression of being wealthy..."

Freddie Mercury – A life in his words

It doesn't matter if you were born in a poor or rich country, that country in the eyes of a child who grew up there, will always be the most beautiful country in the world, especially if he spent a happy childhood surrounded by the love of his family members, like Freddie's and also like mine. Freddie didn't talk about his hometown, but he certainl kept close to himself what was beautiful about that period. I say this because I too grew up in a once very poor but beautiful country, Albania, which is located in the Balkan peninsula. It is a small country bathed by two seas, the Adriatic and the Ionian, crossed internally by the Alps and many rivers that make it even more attractive, together with the main characteristics of the population, which are hospitality and courtesy.

Luckily my parents' work gave us the opportunity to live an adequate life, at least as regards basic needs, making sure that we lacked for nothing. In the 70s, in the Albanian Constitution, Albania proclaimed itself an atheist, so although I knew I came from a Muslim family, no one could be a practitioner of their own religion, because the law categorically forbade it. Although Freddie did not practice the Zoroastrian religion, he was very respectful of his parents who had always been practicing.

I feel like quoting a few lines from the song by Daniele Silvestri *The things we have in common,* because it gives a good idea.

The things we have in common are 4850
I've always counted them...
Only the look is not quite the same
Because mine is usual, but yours is too good
The things we have in common are very easy to spot.
We like loud music...
Let's put on a CD before we fall asleep,
And when we wake up it must be there.

For us fans it is important to have something in common with our idols. It makes us feel closer and more like them. Each of us finds something that brings him closer to the band, such as a birthday date, a hobby, a way of doing, the zodiac sign, a place, a name, a favorite animal, the color of hair and eyes. On the latter, the raven black of the hair and the ebony black of the eyes associate me with Freddie. I think my closeness to him also comes from having many other things in common.

In *Too Much Love Will kill You* (Queen 1988), Freddie sings:

How would it be if you were standing in my shoes?

Placing myself several times in his shoes, I managed to distinguish the elements we had in common and several coincidences of dates. Freddie attended boarding school in India from the age of 8, and faced life alone. When he returned to Zanzibar, at the age of 18, he was forced to change country again due to a revolution, and emigrate to London, exactly to Feltham in Middlesex. In elementary school I attended lessons in the afternoon, and consequently I spent the days alone because my parents and one of my sisters worked in the morning, while my older sister studied in the capital, Tiran, where she stayed in boarding school. There is no comparison between the loneliness I felt seeing my parents only in the evening, and that of Freddie who was very far away, and sometimes didn't even come back for the summer holidays, but I understood it...

For the same reason Bulsara family left Zanzibar, I left my own country at the age of 20. The reason was however a revolution, against the communist regime. Albania had lived in complete isolation, and at that moment the dictatorship was giving way to democracy, and as in every written history, this event never happens through peace. The revolt of young university students changed the country, but a large part of the population was forced to leave and I was one of them. I left my country suddenly, risking my life, precisely six months after my father's sudden and young death, and this was yet another reason to do it, taking into account the strong bond that I had with him.

The moving of Bulsara family took place in 1964 (the year my sister Elida was born, only to die at the age of 39 after a long illness). This is why when I see the photos and videos of Freddie in the last years of his life, his physical but above all psychological suffering touches me closely. It was the suffering of someone who knows that his life is about to end. The opening of the borders in Albania took place on 6 March 1991 (Mary's last birthday with Freddie). Just that day, among soldiers and policemen who prevented the removal of people from the port of Durres to Italy, I embraked with other friends on a fishing boat and after 13 hours of navigation in the sea force 7, on a journey between life and death, I landed late at night in Brindisi. I can only say that I am alive by a miracle. This journey towards freedom marked me so much. I was twenty years old and I never spoke about it to anyone from my home country, I distanced myself from everyone, cousins and friends, just like Freddie had. I never asked why this behavior, and I was not even aware, until the moment I read that he had done the same. It was as if by walking away I wanted to close with everything and everyone and think about what awaited me, my future, another life in another country.

So unfortunately, the year of Freddie's death corresponds to that of my arrival in Italy.

Despite living in London for many years and speaking English perfectly, having also studied it in college, Freddie never acquired the true London accent, to the point that even the actor Rami Malek, who plays him in *Bohemian Rhapsody*, said that he had to work really hard to get an accent like his. Even though thirty years have passed since I resided in Italy, I still have a foreign accent even if I speak it correctly. It will be because it is easier to master the correct pronunciation of a language in childhood than in adolescence. The more I went on reading about him, the more affinity I found. I smiled when I read that he was a stamp collector, because it reminded me of the collection I started when I was in elementary school, but I had no idea where the book in which I put one on each page had ended up, leafing through it often to look and count them. After coming to Italy my mother moved, and unfortunately some childhood memories were lost. Freddie began collecting stamps at the age of 12 and continued as an adult. His collection included stamps from various countries around the world.

Many came from the British Empire, and those of particular philatelic interest from Zanzibar. Also in his album were a large selection of Eastern European stamps, the series of First Day Covers that were issued by the Post Office, and some he gave to the children of his friends.

I later learned that his collection was auctioned off for charity two years after his death, with all profits going to the AIDS organization Mercury Phoenix Trust.

Both Freddie and I as children had sporting skills that often led us to excel. I had an innate speed that came out in various sports that I practiced such as athletics, handball, table tennis and obviously basketball, which I practiced at a high level. Like him, I hated long runs, but in the sprints we were both very fast.

Freddie had protuding teeth, which I honestly like a lot. He never tried to fix this imperfection for his personal reasons, but the self-irony with which he accepted his defect made me understand and accept a different imperfection on my part, and I later decided to remove the dental clamps.

Often Freddie used an ironic and amused communication, accompanying the sentences with his typical laugh and making the others laugh too. This comes out both in the relationship with the other members of the band and with friends, and in the answers he gave to journalists during the interviews. Irony and self-irony are two other things that I have in common with him, who just like me hated wasting time. We are actually two emotional characters.

Listening once more to Queen's vast repertoire, I discovered a song with a slightly Arabic rhythm called *Mustapha*. With the voice of a muezzin in the minaret Freddie "calls" *Mustapha, Ibrahim*, names that correspond to my paternal grandfather, whom I never knew, and to my cousin, my aunt's son. Coincidences of course. Like *Bismillah*, *Mustapha* also recalled the Muslim religion, and the song ends with *"May peace be with you"*. Who knows if he was inspired by his childhood, when he roamed the streets of Bombay among the bazaars and the bizarre melodies of the snake-charmers…

Since I'm on the subject of family, I had read that no one will inherit the surname Bulsara, because Freddie was the last heir, and not having had children, his surname dies with him. My surname will also not be inherited because I am the last heir, and I have neither brothers or male cousins.

I write at night, precisely now it's two o'clock. I sleep little and consider sleep wasted time, in which I could do other important things. Even Freddie thought sleeping was a huge waste of time. He said about this: *"I relax in ways that most people don't understand, like getting 20 minutes of sleep. I don't need hours of sleep."*

As we all know, Freddie's astrological sign is Virgo, with Mercury ruling planet. I, on the other hand, am of the sign of Taurus but with a Virgo ascendant. My father was of his same sign.

"I'm a Virgo, like Greta Garbo, I want to be left alone. I'm a very lonely guy, but I don't do it on purpose."

Freddie Mercury – A life in his words

Those born under the sign of Virgo are very altruistic, they love their work, they are precise and strive for perfection and go forward in their lives making big plans. Those born under this sign have an intelligence above the norm, and a discreet artistic taste. Due to their tendency to be perfectionists and practical sense, they can be entrusted with tasks that require accuracy and precision, being certain that they will complete them in the best possible way. While they are good companions, they tend to be very selfish. These are all characteristics that were part of Freddie's character. He did not accept criticism and when he felt attacked, as Peter Freestone writes with David Evans in *Freddie Mercury – An intimate biography:*

"He acted like a terrier grappling with a big pillow and wouldn't stop biting until he had destroyed it. He always tended to make an elephant out of a fly."

Virgo hates acting in a hurry: never force her to act immediately, she must have time to examine everything coldly, patiently. I am reflected in some qualities such as precision, planning, practical sense, selfishness, and I hardly accept criticism.

Looking at some photos, I came to the conclusion that perhaps Freddie had a great liking for Samantha Fox. I first heard her song *Touch Me* when I was a teenager, and decided to name my first child after her, if it was a girl.

And so it was. Among other things, she was born on the same day and month.

Yellow was the color that Freddie used the most, from shirts to tracksuits, from bathrobes to vests, to jackets, so much so that he reported it in his verses. In *The Fairy Feller's Master-Stroke* (Queen, 1974) he writes:

"The nymph in yellow / you can see the main shot."

The yellow of the lemon tree shouldn't have been missing in his garden and neither in mine (I even insisted on planting one in the garden of the nursery where I work) and the yellow of the lights in the house shouldn't illuminate from above but only with the lampshades, and this also applies to me. The yellow jersey represented me for many years in the basketball championships until my debut in Serie A. I played in the yellow jersey with the number 6, like Mary's date of birth, and I also have the height in common with her, 170 cm. I am a sporty and energetic person like him.

And how can I forget his photo among the yellow daffodils in *I'm Going Slighly Mad (Queen, 1991).*

One thousand and one yellow daffodils
Begin to dance in front of you, oh dear

Freddie loved daffodils and multi-coloured roses. Especially the blue moons. His performances ended with a champagne toast, and the throwing of roses to the audience accompanied by the notes of *God Save the Queen*, the national anthem of the United Kingdom. After his death, members of his English fan club organized a fundraiser to name his favorite flower after him. Rose *Freddie Mercury* is a hybrid tea rose, yellow with apricot nuances towards the tips of the petals. After that, fans decided to send the first specimens of *Rose Freddie Mercury* to his mother, sister Kashmira, life partner Mary Austin, band members and other people who have been close to him.

Now I live in an apartment at number 39, just like the title of the song, but I remember the house where I lived three years ago. House number 6, another coincidence. In the garden I had planted many types of roses, including the one called *Freddie Mercury*, without knowing that it was dedicated to him. I got the bulbs in Albania. I discovered this by carefully re-looking at the photos taken a few years ago.

When, once in the counselor course, our tutor asked *"If you were to identify yourself with a flower or a tree, what would it be and why?"* I replied: *"I would be a red rose. Sweet, fragrant, fiery, but also pungent, difficult to tear off"*. I love roses. I've always preferred them to other flowers just like you, Freddie.

Jer, Freddie's mother, was born on October 16th, just the same day as my older sister, Engjellushe.

On 19 May 1977, my eighth birthday, Queen played the Sporthalle in Basel, Switzerland, the only event in their chronology that matches this date over the years. And speaking of number 19, Deacon and Brian also celebrate their birthdays on 19, respectively August and July, and Mary was 19 when she met Freddie, twenty-four at the time, and better not talk about number 24.

I have often thought about how you would have pronounced my diminutive, Rudi, since you had known people with the same name. One fine day, September 26, 2020, a fan of the group sent me a video, shot in the last year of your life, in which you pronounce my name exactly, sending my heart into fibrillation. Hearing my name pronounced in your delicate voice meant a unique sensation for me. You spoke to Rudi Dolezal, the producer-director very close to you: *"Rudi, are you ready?"*

"I'm very ready" I replied immediately without thinking. Ready to pick pomegranates as a symbol of fertility and lineage of the cult of Zoroaster, or have a nice game of ping-pong with you.

***

All these commonalities, happenings, preferences and coincidences brought me a lot closer to Freddie. Like me many fans find several things in common with him:

"I have a common birth date with Freddie, September 5th."

"Self-irony."

"I don't have many things in common with Freddie, but like him I consider myself an honest person who believes in true friendship, that for me is sacred, and then like Freddie I can seem exuberant, but deep down I'm very shy and reserved, and I open up with very few people, only with those I consider close friends, as he called them."

"The Zodiac sign."

"I also play the piano like him. Without making comparisons of course."

"I have similar views on life. Also, judging by the app based on the similarity of the faces in the photo, there is 32% similarity between him and me, but I don't know whether that's true or not."

***

And the people all stared didn't understand
But you knew my name on sight
Oh, whatever came of you and me
      Now I'm here (Queen, 1979)

***

"У меня схожие с ним мнения и некоторые взгляды на жизнь. А также , судя по приложению по сходству лиц по фотографии, у меня показывает 32 процента сходства между ним и мной, вот только не знаю правда или нет".

FREDDIE'S PERSONALITY ACCORDING TO THE ENNEAGRAM

"You always have a certain idea of what you are like, and I think my character on stage is completely different from that off stage. Inside me there are different facets. I'm generally easygoing I guess, but I can change and being moody and obnoxious. I believe any personality is made up of a lot of ingredients, and I'm no different. I don't take half measures, which can be risky because people can take advantage of me, which has happened many times. But then in certain situations I'm a sex object, big and macho, and I'm very arrogant. And then, no one can put their feet on my head."
Freddie Mercury – Words and thoughts

Many biographers have tried to understand what Freddie Mercury's personality was like. Judged for his excesses and reckless life, with his being reserved he became a mystery to be unraleved, because the character and the person were two different worlds.

The books I read helped me better understand his character, made up of a set of qualities that took him to the top. I even unwinded the interviews so that I could read them several times, and I saw all the videos that also showed him in relation to other people.

Having become passionate about the Enneagram after having attended several courses on the subject, I came to the conclusion that Freddie was a character 2, which has the capital vice of pride as its basis. I compared myself with other people with more knowledge in the field to get confirmations, and that's how I was sure that he was part of that group of personalities. I thought that for us fans it could be an extra tool to fully understand his behavior, his way of being and doing, and his defese mechanisms towards the outside world.

For those who don't know what the Enneagram is, I would like to briefly explain it with a few simple words. It is a psychological tool that helps to identify the type of personality, to get to know oneself and others better, to understand our experiences, and helps us to understand our strengths and weaknesses by assuming more awareness, in order to be able to better manage our emotions and relationships, and to be able to improve, accept ourselves as well as others.

Enneagram is a word from the Greek, formed by *ennea* (nine), and *gram* (drawing), therefore, 9-point drawing. The true origins of the Enneagram are said to date back some 2,000 years, and was an approach afferent to Sufi mystics. In the early 1900s it was introduced in Europe by the Russian Gurdjieff. But it was after the 1960s that this instrument was developed by Oscar Ichazo and Claudio Naranjo (my teacher), in order to study personality and character. Character is a cage and this powerful psychological tool helps to get out of it after becoming aware of ourselves.

There are nine characters in the world, each divided into three subtypes. This theory is based on the seven deadly sins (which are those that do not allow us to see reality), plus the character 6 (fear) and 9 (self-forgetfulness), and it's used as a map in psychology.

Characters 2 (pride), 3 (vanity) and 4 (envy) are emotional. Characters 5 (greed), 6 (fear) and 7 (gluttony) are thought characters. Characters 8 (lustria), 9 (self-forgetfulness) and 1 (anger) are part of the instinctive sphere. All characters are divided into three sub-types: social, conservative and sexual, which despite having the same capital vice, are different from each other.

All of us fans know Freddie's life perfectly, so I wouldn't want to repeat myself, but I would just like to dwell on character 2 of the sexual subtype, to better understand his way of being and doing. Character 2 basically has pride, which is considered the main sin, and needs to be recognized as indispensable for the other without being aware of how much he is on the opposite side. For example this comes out in the relationship with Jim Hutton and beyond. In Queen his presence was essential.

Within the family, the Enneatype 2 child represents a source of joy and happiness. Freddie was his parents' delight. In childhood this character was able to cope with pain, taking refuge in fantasies and imagination. As a child he was denied his needs, and consequently when he grows up he does everything to reach the top, especially when he comes from a non-rich family, managing to react to a lack. This phase corresponds with his childhood spent at St. Peter's School in Bombay, India, and later on all the way he has done go get to have a prominent career.

"Obviously, I had the impression that I had been sent away from my parents and sister, who I missed very much. I felt alone, I felt like I was rejected" says Freddie, perhaps expressing his sense of abandonment.

2 is an emotional character, in need of love, with a great capacity for seduction, always conquering people without really wondering if they are interested in him. The idea of not being abandoned as a unique friend or companion, is maifested by placing oneself at the center of attention. As far as feelings are concerned, he is extroverted to the point of feeling special and adorable for the others and he uses rationality to promote his image, creating an internal paradise of fullness. His delicate and flexible body affirms the tendency to establish erotic and affectionate relationships, which is one of the main characteristics of this Ennatype.

"Mine are commercial love songs and I like to put my emotional touch on them. I write songs like this because after all, what I feel strongly is love, it's emotion" said Freddie admitting he was emotional. In fact, being a

character in touch with emotions, often in the letters he sent to his parents when he was in college, he was able to describe both his negative and positive emotions. In a letter dated March 15, 1962, he wrote that he was very angry that Bruce had started hitting him, and even if he didn't want to, a boxing match had inevitably started. After describing what had happened in minute detail, he kept expressing other strong emotions saying he was so sad and furious. But when he won *Best All Rounder Junior* throphy, he said he was very proud and hoped they were too.

This character is attracted to the good things in life, but at the same time terrified of boredom and heaviness. The confirmation are the words of Freddie when he points out the use of different recording studios to change the environment or in entrusting his music to Jim Beach.

"Do what you want with my music, but don't make me boring", considering his music not a precious commodity, but a consumer product, and pointing out that his main topics are love and emotions. This character needs continuous passionate stimuli, he convince and seduce with language, by matching strategic seduction with beautiful speech. He is moved in expressing true emotions and consequently feels a sense of modesty, which makes him shy and reserved.

The 2 are nice, intelligent, brilliant, cheerful and pleasant, they make people laugh and love to laugh back, they make others feel good and give them moral support. Who better than Freddie can confirm these characteristics. We have seen many videos in which he laughs and jokes, even in the recording room or in interviews, and even in the last videos in which he had become fully aware of his destiny, he found the courage to be sunny as always. Plus they are friendly people. He liked friendship, so much so that he had decided to live in the same house surrounded by friends. They are attracted by power and fame, but being cheerful and spirited, they are consequently sought after by opposite, melancholy and pessimistic characters. With their effervescent temperament they arouse the appreciation of others.

The main defense mechanism is the transformation of anger into an obsessive-compulsive drive. Freddie had stated several times that, especially after a furious argument, he managed to compose songs quickly enough, and it was as if he was looking for the conflict to be more creative. Another defense mechanism is removal. In this case Paul Prenter comes to mind. With his statements to the *Sun* in May 1987 he unleashed the fury of Freddie Mercury and consequently his removal. The same thing also happened with the Trident record company, for how he had managed their contract by entering into a conflict of interest. After the transfer of relations with Trident, Freddie declared:

"As far as we are concerned, our old management is dead. For us it no longer exists, in any way...And we feel quite relieved."

Lesley-Ann Jones, *I Will Rock You*

His anger and wounded pride can be heard in *Death on Ttwo Legs* (Queen, 1975), a song dedicated to the Trident record company.

Now you can kiss my ass goodbye -
Was the fin on your back part of the deal? Shark

To then continue again with *Flick of the Whrist*.

Baby, you've been had
Intoxicate your brain with what I'm saying
If not, you'll lie in knee-deep trouble

This personality exalts his own charm and value, confirming pride as the basic capital vice, therefore the claim to deserve a privileged position by any means. We all know that Freddie, while he was still in the early stages of his career, said *"I will not be a star, I will be a legend"*.

Being people simply in love with themselves, passionate, energetic, rebellious to any kind of resistance, they show an insistent search for pleasure and the need to be loved erotically, thus revealing a characteristic of this character which is the hedonism. Often Freddie admitted his excesses in the pursuit of sex, but also the need to be loved. A central feature of type 2 is histrionics, which consists of attracting attention by showing the emphasized expression of emotion. These individuals are extremely bold and self-confident. They believe they are a fortune and a resource for those around them. They are proud to feel special, and for this reason they believe they deserve attention and privilieges.

Freddie is a sexual subtype of character 2 and therefore

the most seductive of all. This personality has a soft and persuasive language. It is no coincidence that in his book *Experiences of Transformation with the Enneagram,* the anthropologist Claudio Naranjo describes this enneatype exactly like this:

"A glamorous and beautiful femme fatale but with a dangerous beauty, who needs to grab you and could end up devouring you. They aspire to be irresistible until they unleash the greatest passions. The sexual 2 therefore shows us that it is possible to believe that, inspiring a great passion, is a way to resolve everything in life."

Other adjectives suitable for this character are: ambitious, competitive, brilliant, creative, energetic, outgoing, available, adventurous, free, stubborn, theatrical, capricious and self-confident. At times he has mood swings (he himself admits in *A life in his own words* that he is a man with mood swings), but he is also vain, (*"I know I'm still beautiful"*), he feels a sense of shame and loves children. In *These Are the Days of Our Lives* (Queen, 1991) he expresses it through these lines:

When life was just a game

There is no point in sitting and thinking about what you have done
When you can lay back and enojy it through your children

In a video in which Mary is holding Roger's daughter, little Rory, Freddie approaches and lifts the collar of her shirt, stroking it gently.

"The best deal was made by Little Freddie, who found himself with a terribly affectionate, loving and extremely generous godfather. That godfather, Freddie, shared birthdays, family dinners and a real home away from home with us."

"Once I overheard a conversation between him and my son Felix. Freddie was saying to him: «I haven't had the luck you have. When I was little I spent many years in boarding school, away from mum and dad». With my children he spoke a lot about his childhood. He loved children. As soon as they were able to walk and talk and answer, they liked being with him."

Reinhold Mack

The testimonies and statements of his record producer confirm the concept.

In this enneatype, the natural physical constitution is delicate and graceful, but if it gets fat it tends to take on harmonious shape. Actually towards the years '87-'88, despite a few extra pounds, Freddie was always in perfect shape, and those extra pounds didn't change his physiognomy.

This character is not interested in educated theories or political ideas, facts and calculations, but is interested in dealing with interpersonal relationships and daily life. In several interviews Freddie declares that Queen have never expressed political ideas in their songs. Ready to give moral support, he is more interested in the visual aspect than in the judgments of others, managing to cut the negative judgment out of himself. Reserved in private but with an effervescent temperament, he seeks to arouse appreciation in others. Freddie has always admitted that he liked being in love, but this was not a weakness; on the contrary, he was capable of making decisions. In love he wanted to dominate: this type of character, in fact, unconsciously prefers men or women with less money and power and not particularly educated, to have control of the situation.

His over the top personality, free and unconventional, gave him an incredibly powerful stage presence. The relationship with money is expressed in the fact that money is not for survival, but for love.

His being determined and direct, means that the comparisons sometimes become quite heated. This has repeatedly led Freddie to have quarrels with other artists as in the case of Sid Vicious, bassist and leader of Sex Pistols, because Freddie could not conceive of a muscial genre like punk.

Being the "terminator" of problems, they immediately take action to make them disappear. Projected towards the future, for them there is always time for the problems they avoid, and in fact even Freddie, avoiding talking about his disease to his parents and thinking about it, continued to do his job as before until the end, thus also avoiding the pain it caused him. It happens until the last song, *Mother Love*: exhausted and powerless, he never admitted to suffering and never complained of the pain he felt. He even promised Brian to go back to the studio, which he couldn't do, thus leaving the guitarist to continue the second and last part of the song.

Obviously this is a small description according to my understanding of this theory, but as Freddie said *"I don't talk to anyone, so they don't know the real me, nor will they"*. In part it will always be like this.

***

December 29, 2019

Ad administrator asks: *"Who is Freddy Mercury to me? I offer you this reflection which is not a survey or a game, but a way to express our love for this great man and artist. Write us in the comments what our beloved Bad Guy represents for you"*. Here are some of the answers:

"For me Freddie is magic, from every point of view: his music, his voice, his charisma, his physicality. Everything about him is real magic that envelops you and never leaves you."

"Freddie is music, dancing, singing. Freddie is love, kindness, altruism, passion, elegance and ease. Freddie was a good man, he was he, nothing more."

"Freddie for me is an idol, an example, a reference, the strength, the courage, the loyalty, the genius. And of course Love, Love made person. I believe in Angels and I am deeply convinced that he is one of them."

"For me he is an example of courage, passion, inner beauty (in addition to the physical one). A constant and overbearing presence in my life."

"For me Freddie is my entire adult life, I first heard Queen at the age of 15, I can't imagine life without the music of Queen and Freddie now, because his voice evokes indescribable emotions and sensations in me. I adore his face, body, clothing and everything related to him. I love him for life."

***

"Excess is in my nature and I really need danger and thrills."

"I believe in personality, not newspapers."

Freddie Mercury – A life in his words

> Yes, I'm everybody's Mr Bad Guy
> Can't you see, I'm Mr Mercury
> *Mr Bad Guy* (Freddie Mercury, 1985)

YOUR ABSENCE AND YOUR ESSENCE

"I'm one of those people who doesn't look back and cries over spilled milk."
Freddie Mercury – A life in his words

August 27, 2020

I was returning from my country, when as the days went by I began to feel bad. I had caught Covid, quite eavily. There were days when I felt like I was dying and I couldn't breathe. The pain in my chest was very strong. I wanted to continue writing, but I was unable to do anything. In those moments I thought about who was really fighting against an evil. I thought of you, Freddie, and more than one question rose spontaneously: How did you manage to sing until your last days? Where did you find the strength to defy pain without ever compaining? Where have you found the courage to stand in front of the cameras lately?

I had always avoided watching the latest videos of the band, because seeing Freddie so different hurt me. Instead at that moment, thinking back on it, his showing himself with dignity, showing the state in which the disease had brought him, just to give the last songs to music and to the people who cared so much, gave me courage.

I watched the video of *These Are the Days of Our Lives* (Queen, 1991). I saw his face and body and asked myself: How did it feel to know your destiny? What did you feel? How did you react? What did you say to the closest people? How did you deal with it? I saw you laughing and joking until the end and this was the best answer to my questions.

The harsh acceptance of reality, your saving your family members from suffering, the desire to continue to do your job to the end in order to leave us an unprecedented musical richness until your last breath, made you go forward courageously. Tell me if we shouldn't treasure these values.

You left with the last *"I still love you"* and with a smile for your fans, who do not give peace, who do not accept your enormous loss, who are unable to mourn even if you we repeat that in your short life you had lived to the fullest, but every now and then we think curiously about how it would have been, how you would have been and what new songs you would have composed. And we feel an unbearable pain knowing that there is no return, but a memory that lives inside each of us and that we keep alive for you every single day. Really miss you so much. A wound that doesn't heal. A void that only your songs fill, but when nostalgia takes over, we feel sad, because we would like to relive a moment from the past and we wish you were alive, and paradoxically we feel happy because your past is always present.

You never felt sorry for yourself or gave up, and you never closed in on yourself. Without ever complaining, with admirable fortitude, you gave your best until the last day, in the face of those who criticized and judged you, teaching humanity a lesson. You have taken control of your destiny and defeated death. You laughed in the face of death, you challenged it by continuing to compose, to sing for yourself and for us, and you celebrated your birthday as if it weren't your last. She couldn't bend you even for a moment. Triumphantly you literally crumbled it under your feet, and you made yourself immortal just like that phoenix you chose for Queen logo. In your way of doing there was a tenacity to live that was stronger than all storms.

Freddie was attending Ealing Art College, graphic arts, when he decided to create a Queen logo, in which the dominant figure was the phoenix, the sacred bird of mythology similar to a golden eagle but with splendid colors: blue, yellow, light blue, red, black and pink.

Many times I asked myself: why the phoenix? And why with low wings? Perhaps because it represented the soul of the sun God, called Ra, or because it heralded a new period of wealth and fertility that would come after so many difficulties? I'll never know for sure, although whatever it was, it was auspicious, and brought him good luck. The motto of the phoenix is *"Post fata resurgo"*, which means

"after death I get up again".

In Greek mythology, there was only one phoenix at a time. It was always a male and lived near a fresh water source, and every morning it bathed and sang such a wonderful song that the sun God stopped his boat. When the phoenix realized that it had reached the end of its days, it retreated to an isolated place, just like you retreated to your beloved Garden Lodge. It is also said that from the phoenix's throat came the breath of new life, a young phoenix destined to live as long as its former one. That's why sometimes we say "to be a phoenix" to indicate something whose equal is unknown, unobtainable, but above all a unique speciment. A mythological bird, which never dies and flies far, and with its absolute beauty creates an incredible sublimation, combined with the dreamlike vision of immortality, also expressing the power of resilience, or the ability to face and overcome the difficulties in a positive way, finding resources found within oneself, cultivating self-esteem, accepting and reacting to every situation however difficult it may be.

Like the phoenix you sang beautiful songs and you were unique, unparalleled and daring. You have identified yourself in the phoenix. You are the phoenix. Symbol of resilience, strength and physical endurance. Dying to be reborn and become a legend, because while death took possession of your body, you took possession of eternity.

We firmly believe that you are somewhere, only in this way we can ease the pain, and we dream that you can somehow see us, see the creativity of us fans: stories, poems, crochet work, paintings, drawings and other creations that make your gaze real.

We are in contact with each other through the phrases dedicated to you every day, and we live through your timeless songs. All of us together in front of a monitor to follow live performances for the thousandth time, concerts as if we were all there, listening to infinity, because your image in our minds is and will always be that of a young, beautiful, noble, elegant and talented boy with Parsi traits.

You worked hard to achieve your dream of becoming a singer, but for us you are so much more, you are our *great pretender*, a musician of value and substance, a transformer-performer, a baritone, a super-talent, an artist with the most powerful voice in history, a genius, a leader who has become a myth.

In the video clip of *I'm Going Slightly Mad* you compare yourself to Edith Piaf, and certainly the personality was similar, radiant, multi-faceted, very cultured and theatrical, and because despite the problems, you had a lot of fun and no regrets. You didn't have much time left, but you asked for some material to sing so that the others could finish it, because you loved working and it wasn't only worth listening to you but also looking at you, a spectacle of nature.

Some verses of his songs are testimony of his "unconscious prophecy", or simply of his intuition. It was as if he foresaw the future, as if he had a presentiment of his destiny, a premonition, even simply of a symbolic death from suffering for a love gone wrong.

In *Bohemian Rhapsody* in 1975 he sings: *"Too late, my time has come…my body aches all the time…I don't want to die…So you think you can love me and then let me die."*

In 1974 in *Seven Seas of Rhye:* *"Lord do and I will die".*

In 1975 in *God Save the Queen:* *"God save the Queen. You got it right we love our Queen".* But God wanted to keep you in the bosom of the gods.

In *Somebody to Love* in 1976 he sings: *"Every morning I get up and die a little...I barely stand...I take a look in the mirror and cry...Lord, what are you doing to me?"*

In 1976, in *You Take My Breath Away* he says exactly these words: *"I would surely die."*

1978, *Jealousy:* *"But it doesn't matter if I have to live or die."*

And continuing with *Hammer to Fall*, written with Brian May, in 1984 Freddie sings:
A little piece of you is falling away
Build your muscles as your body decays yeah
Let the anaesthetic cover it all

Instead in 1985 in the amazing version of *Made in Heaven* in his solo album he sings:
I'm taking my right with destiny
And in *The March of the Black Queen:*
Like going up to heaven and then coming back alive

And all your *"Let me go"* in various songs, as if you were asking to be let go, not to suffer, not to be judged, to live your life in complete freedom, because time waits for no one, to come back in the womb every time the word "mother" was pronounced in one of your songs.

A short life, but fully lived as many lives put together. Enthusiastic and cheerful, excessive and brilliant, you dedicated yourself to music until the end of your days, because you are the Music, the one that even after almost thirty years is listened to and sang with emphasis, still imagining you on stage with the flags of your host countries waving as you ran, with the red cape and the king's crown, like in your last concert at Knebworth Park, when you thanked your audience. You called us "beautiful people", you said good night and a huge "we love you". You know we love you too, Freddie. It was physically your last time on stage, but I'm sure you'll be giving another concert on a stage suspended in the air, like our breath when we hear you sing.

Like a *deus ex machina* you have given a solution to a situation that is now irresolvable, complicated and with no way out. You, the God descended to earth, have ignored cause and effect, and without regrets and repentance, you had done what you wanted in your life, and at the most difficult moment you went on as if nothing had happened. It was worth it having given us your heart and soul, having lived on ballads and rock'n'roll, having made us move, having made us feel strong emotions that still accompany us every day. Your spiritual legacy, the most precious asset, the music you left us has a safe place, it lives inside the coundless love of your fans. And while the press was chasing you, while experiencing enormous suffering, you supported AIDS research to charitable organizations, humbly and without declaring it publicly, just like when you wrote a check to those in need.

That cursed Sunday of November 24, 1991 was your last day on this earth. Music mourned its master and still mourns him, and fans unable to hold back the pain filled the sidewalk in front of Garden Lodge with flowers, bouquets, tickets and banners. Time stopped. You decided to give your breaths to all of us, to make us live with true music. You, good, generous and humble soul. The phoenix had lifted its head and wings to fly into the sky, towards a new home in the constellation of your Solar System zodiac sign, between Mars and Jupiter in the asteroid 17473 which coincidentally was discovered in the same year as your farewell to the world, and bears your name. They say it reflects the light that strikes it, but I would say that it shines with its own light, and warmth can be felt down here, together with the love you distribute.

***

And since everything I seek from life I find in your *"C'est la vie"*, you continue to ask us: "Oh, how are things on earth?", and we will answer you like this:

"I close my eyes and if it weren't for your last photos, in which your body was worn out, you walked with difficulty, the testimonies of your death, the funeral. I dream that you are alive somewhere in the world, enjoying life, having extravagant parties as only you were capable of doing, as only you were able to live the moments. Sometimes it is so difficult for me to imagine that you are no longer here, precisely because you loved living so much, as that plaque on your statue in Montreux says: singer of songs, lover of life. Then I open them again and listen to your voice, your notes on the worn out CD."

"For those who loved him and still love him, it is not enough that he lives only in hearts."

"He's a legend, and legends never die."

"He will forever remain in our hearts."

"Only those who love him deeply, can understand the importance of his music, and his example in the life of each of us. We miss you so much."

"He bequeathed his songs and his beautiful voice."

"People we love never leave. They embrace us with the wind, support us with tears of rain, protect us with the warmth of the sun and look at us through the stars and speak to us: with a number, a feather, or a heart."

"If only he was among us. I think he'd be happy to see how much the old and new generation love him."

"I cannot tell you how sad this picture makes me feel. As I think this was his last recording of singing, and his health had deteriorated so much. He was the strongest person I know having battled this awful disease, but just kept right on going until the very end. Much respect for this unbelievably talented legend".

"Es increible que nos haya dejado; pero con su musica tengo esa sensacion de que esta vivo. Lo extraño y lo amo!" *"It's incredible that he left us; but with his music I have the feeling that he is alive. I miss him and I love him."*

"Every now and then I close my eyes to immerse myself in a world of memories, of moments that will never come back: the remembrance of Freddie in life, of his enchanted voice that accompanied my youth; a magical road opens up to the heart: a road made of past and present emotions. I dare say eternal towards this artist who has made his life an incredible show. Passion, love, esteem. I wish I could scream for him to hear: thank you Freddie dear, immensely immense, thank you for being in my life, because only memory is stronger than love. I remind you that it is not a lack but a shining presence."

"In addition to his music, he has left us his strength and his example of tenacity and of never wanting to give up, even when your hopes are nil."

"You did it for us. You loved us until strength accompanied you on your painful last journey. And we reciprocate this love with so much passion that I'm sure it reaches up there, among the stars where you are."

***

"We miss him and love him, may God be with him always."

Jer Bulsara, Freddie's mother

"Life is very short to sit around and think about it."
Freddie Mercury – A life in his words

So I live to the fullest, yes I live to the fullest
And I give my all, and I give my all
I Want It All (Queen, 1989)

THE GHOST TRACK

"No, actually I don't care much, in fact I really don't care at all. I have no aspirations of wanting to live to be seventy, really. I don't want to sound like an exaggeration, but, I mean, I know I'm forty-one and seventy is a long way off, and I don't give a damn. And as far as I'm concerned I've lived a full life, and if I'm dead tomorrow, I really don't give a damn. I really have already done everything. I love that I can make people happy in any form, you know? I make them happy. Even if it's for half an hour of their live, if there's a way I can make them feel lucky and bring a smile to a forlorn face, it will be worth it to me"

Freddie Mercury (David Wigg interview)

If I had to describe the emotions that each song leaves me, I would need winter days and endless sheets. Precisely for this reason I choose to describe and interpret in my own way an unusual, different, enigmatic and profound piece that takes me to the place that Freddie wanted to take in the sky.

It is extraordinarily make in heaven, track number 13, called *Track 13, Ghost track* or *New Age Ambiance*, known as *Ghost Track*, apparently absent in the album *Made in Heaven*. I find in it something spiritual. I believe that it was not accidental to put it at number 13, perhaps there was a very specific thought of Brian, Roger and John behind it, and if this was not the case, it still coincides perfectly with the meaning of this number in numerology. This number represents the alchemist (he who practiced alchemy), a philosophical system that manifests itself through the language of various disciplines such as physics, chemistry, astrology, medicine, metallurgy, leaving numerous marks in the history of art. It occurs to me that more or less every member of the band was drawn to one of these studies. The first aim of the alchemist was to transform lead into gold. In a metaphorical sense Queen did it with their music. They were quick-changers starting from their stage costumes, their off-stage look and above all in changing musical genres, making many of their songs real valuable pieces. Among the first to make video clips, they began that November 10, 1975, with *Bohemian Rhapsody*, creating a new musical language. Furthermore, the number 13 embodies the origin of the irremediability of change, and is a warning not to cling to what no longer supports evolution.

The *Ghost Track*, with its 22 minutes and 32 seconds, is an original call to the senses, and its notes took me to another parallel world, involving me in a strange extra-terrestrial dimension. I had heard of it, but as the name itself says, something escaped me, because it doesn't appear on the cover of *Made in Heaven*, thus making it even more mysterious. And yet it is there, at the bottom majestically like a book without captions, all to be interpreted, each in its own way, like all the songs of the band.

Sleepless, I decided for the first time to listen to it at three in the morning. The headphones isolated me from reality, making me perceive the sound in such a profound way that I almost lost track of space and time. I closed my eyes to completely immerse myself and fully appreciate its significance. I was no longer in the "here and now", I was elsewhere, in an unknown world with the clamorous continuous sound and I tried to let go, obtaining the opposite effect. The multiplicity of instruments seemed a mix between a scream and a cry, to then continue with a sound like bells on the background of an unchanged music that intrigued me a lot. That prolonged sound from various musical devices had the appearance of a voice that slowly lowered, almost dying out. I felt restless, but kept listening to that internal battle that ended with the piano notes in A

E A flat. At 10:32 mark Freddie's space voice came suddenly and I felt a shiver run down my spine. There was nothing earthly in his voice asking *"Are You Running?"* nine times, and seemed to descend from the mountain to sink into the lake, to then continue with a linear music that echoed on the surface. His voice mixed with some strange percussion, making me feel his immortal spirit. I remained motionless with my heart in my throat waiting to hear it again, but after a while the sound began to be similar to that of a vortex that sucks everything in: thoughts, actions, problems, affections, loves, a whole life. At minute 13:15 a kind of clock, with a high and low rhythm, began a "tic toc" that mingled with the beating of my heart, as if to warn that the time had arrived. I heard it banging wildly, but the bells that rang again soothed him like rattles hanging from a newborn's crib.

The awe was inevitable, yet I let myself get caught up in the moment. Subsequently, an acoustic effect halfway between a burst and a low-pitched whistle, seemed to warn of the peace achieved through the note E. I experienced strange mystical sensations, difficult to decipher. It was like fighting in the iceberg of the unconscious, where two thirds of everything is found in depth, in that part that is not aware and that you cannot explain.

At minute 19:53, the surprising laugh of Mercury, the God with wings on his feet had taken flight, helped by that wind that personified him and freed himself forever from suffering, that name that suits you so much, with your intellectual and communicative faculties, sense of humor and rationality, you have fully represented. Finally through mysterious sounds one last time his voice affirmed emphatically *"Fab" (Fabulous)*, and fabulously concluded his earthly journey, reaching the sky.

"People can you hear me, give me a sign, because I want it now, I Want It All Now."

***

"This track soothes me after crying through the other songs. I feel it's Freddie's ascension into heaven that brings me some peace knowing his suffering is over."

"A fabulous flight, wonderful music in full new age style and a laugh and a word that come from another dimension. Freddie is finally free."

> *This life that lasts for a thousand years*
> *It will soon end*
> *Magic, it's a kind of magic*
> *A Kind of Magic* (Queen, 1986)

> *Yes, I'm a rocket ship on my way to Mars*
> *Don't Stop Me Now* (Queen, 1979)

HOW I IMAGINE YOU TODAY…

"One way or another I'm going to try to stay in the music industry, because that's all I know how to do, really."
Freddie Mercury – A life in his words

When for the first time I read Cesare Cremonini's preface to Luca Garrò's biography of Freddie Mercury, I liked it very much. I found it very heartfelt and real. With each of his descriptions, I tried to place Freddie in the environment to which he belonged. As soon as I finished reading it, I asked myself: how do I imagine him today?

Certainly still composing music and exploring new territories, certainly transmitting his values and teaching the new generations how to achieve success, giving tips and advice. Brilliant as you were, you would always be on the go and full of new ideas, one of which I see come true like this…

At London Coliseum, in one of the largest theaters in London, the curtain opens for an operatic recital intertwined with the musical.

In the semi-darkness of the crowded room, we notice the harmonious silhouette of a man in his seventies; smiling face, cultured beard, lean physique and short gray hair. After having given the last directions to the young sopranos and baritones, he hurriedly down the side stairs and sat down in first row, to attend the singular show he staged with so much dedication and passion. Occasionally he speaks in a low voice and laughs with the two women next to him, but then concentrates on what is happening on stage. After so many years he hasn't lost his habit of irony.

The work in progress is the story of a life marked by music, but also by internal conflicts, loneliness, changes of mind, fame and success. Accompanied by a large symphony orchestra positioned below the stage, the show begins. But the absolute protagonist is that white piano, which accompanies all the artists individually. In front of the technological panorama of the crystalline sea of Nakupenda, a happy child recites and dances. Then the screen shows the streets of Bombay. The child plays with a hockey stick and throws the ball which disappears under the piano, but while he goes looking for it in the semi-darkness, he transforms into a teenager who surprises with his way of playing unknown melodies, in front of a background of 70s London. As soon as he exits, another singer enters from the opposite side, a thin but talented boy, who enchants the audience with his voice and look.

The path of growth as a musician continues with a potpourri of beautiful songs that go back so many years ago. A stupendous vocal metamorphosis, and an adult who surprises the non-stop applauding audience. The set of violins makes events flow, and a flute voice similar to that of the diva Montserrat Caballè, guest of honor of the evening, recalls the precise moment of collaboration and complicity with Freddie Mercury. The first two verses of the chorus, *How Can I Go On*, and the music changes course, followed by a huge ensemble of voices.

And finally a simulation of Wembley, the live performance, which has gone down in history for its majesty.

On his face and in his gestures we understand the satisfaction for having reached another goal, always remaining faithful to his great passion, music, and always giving his all in what he did best.

With opera, which you had already intertwined with rock, your life is now a unique work of its kind. You. Like Verdi, Bellini, Donizetti, Rossini and the great composers you loved so much, bring back to the fore the musical genre par excellence, created only by ingenious minds. You are there, satisfied to give an example of your success earned with so much work, as a witness of excellence in teaching kids to achieve their goals with enthusiasm, stimulating their work. You're doing what you envisioned doing: you've totally succeeded. You have always gone beyond the schemes, and you are doing it brilliantly even now, giving unprecedented emotions to everyone present, and to all the fans who have always appreciated you.

The lights come back on. Under the spotlights, your white tuxedo reflects the light, placing you even more at the center of the world. You say thank you and raise your fist in the air as a sign of another victory. Freddie Mercury, you are still among your fans, adored and so loved. You didn't want to repeat the same formula, but always do different things. You wanted to be creative, and you outdid yourself.

The emotion in his eyes is covered by the inseparable Ray Bans. He leaves the theater with a quick step, accompanied by his real friends, Monserrat and Mary.

I see you return to Garden Lodge and as you open the door, your beloved exotic felines surround you and purr.

This is how I imagine your life now, calm, and with your rituals: Thursday at your parents' to taste your mum's biscuits, an occasional party with a small circle of friends, or a lunch all together in the garden, from where I hear your unfailing laughter.

With your confidentiality, a distinctive element of your character, you rarely appear on social networks, but the few times you do, you have all the fans glued in front of a display, asking you questions and comments to which you, as always, with kindness reply.

A long time ago you expressed a desire to do interesting things that you had never done before, or hadn't done in a long time. And here you are choosing the colors for your paintings, like the time you saw the drawing of the French impressionist painter Matisse, and you reproduced it in a short time, identical to the original. I see you inside that room you dedicated to painting, with the walls full of colors, trying your hand at another portrait. The complete artist in you emerges, along with your old passion for painting and drawing that wasn't just limited to paintings. Who knows what else you have in mind?

Surely you haven't lost your passion for antiques. Your refined tastes have remained so, even in the most adult age. And it is also for this reason that I see you with pleasure spending most of your time in your home in absolute privacy. But the favorite is always the music room, where your piano is, where your dancing hands elegantly clap the keyboard, and where you compose new songs to take them around to countries you've never been to, in China, Albania, Russia, in the Greek islands, but always with Japan in the heart. Concerts have remained the beating heart of your career, continuing to make people happy, feel good and print a smile that erases sadness. However it would have gone, I can't help picturing you up and down the stage. There is no space in this globe for you to cultivate pomegranates and make socks for sailors. Music gave birth to you and you honored it. You lived to the fullest and made some wonderful things.

***

April 2, 2020 at 11:35 am. Others imagine him like this...

"Last night I watched the documentary about Queen and Freddie on Rai 5. Although I have recorded them all, when I watch them it is always as if it were the first time. I never miss a word or an expression, and no one is allowed to disturb me. But the real problem is the days that follow. On the one hand, looking at them gives me an indescribable charge and energy, but on the other I'm starting to ask myself questions: if he were still there, what would he be like today? Would he still sing, would he still live in London or even Montreux? And so on. Unanswered questions of course. And then the sadness of

why such a selfless, beautiful and elegant man died like this. What questions do you have about Freddie today?"

"I believe that he would not have wanted to live longer, to grow old. The last masterpieces he made in my opinion, he got there just living those last moments. True masterpieces come out only in the deepest sadness. I don't know if he would have done more if he hadn't had that push in his soul that he had just when he was sick. He was a miraculous comet that passed over the earth. But just a special comet because it is a glow in the dark. If he were still alive, he wouldn't have been a comet."

"In my opinion he would have continued to explore other avenues. Surely if he were alive he wouldn't be considered a legend."

"It is not possible to get higher than he. He still had so much music to give us. Today, I would imagine him in Montreux painting on the banks of the lake."

"In my opinion, if he were still alive, he would compete with Mick Jagger, lively and always on stage."

"I ask myself the exact same questions every time I see the documentaries, but also when I listen to the songs. Lately I've been wondering: I wonder if right now he would have kept us company with an Instagram live while he played the piano."

"He would never be old because there was always a flame of energy inside him that led him to explore new things. This flame accompanied him until the last song."

"Honestly, I would have liked to see his live as they are always very spectacular. Surely he would have continued, too talented to sit still."

"He would have given us some more extraordinary music, most likely he would have pressed Monsty a little longer and they would have unleashed other musical marvels such as Barcelona album.*"*

"I often wonder what relationship he would have with social networks and with today's crazy society. But

I'm sure he would have given the world still great masterpieces...but that's another story."

"Maybe he wouldn't have kept jumping on stage but he would still have given us so much beautiful music with his enchanting, more mature voice."

"Music... Who knows what else he could have written."

"I imagine him as a baritone writing lyric."

"Surely he would have given a hard time to all the others, but fate wanted him to be insurmountable, a legend, always the first in the standings."

***

"Maybe I could go into production or keep writing songs, because I might not be able to run on stage anymore, but still keep composing music. So one way or another music will always be a part of my life."

Freddie Mercury - A life in his words

Take me to the room where red is all red
Take me to the room where green is all green
And from what I've observed it's energizing is fantastic
Take me to the room where rhythm is all around
I'm gonna tear that sound apart(yeah, yeah, yeah)
Dragon Attack (Queen, 1980)

A WEEKEND AT THE DUCK HOUSE

October 30 – November 2, 2020 (Friday, Saturday, Sunday and Monday)

Lazing around on a Sunday afternoon
Friday I'm going to paint at...
I'm forced to propose on a Saturday night
I'll be lounging around on a Sunday
I leave for work on Monday mornings
Lazing on a Sunday Afternoon (Queen)

We are not born with passions, but we make them ours when something or someone strikes us, for example by looking at a famous painting and dreaming of becoming a painter, looking at a touching photo and thinking of becoming good photographers, reading a poem with the hope of writing one ourself, listening to music and buying a guitar with the desire to learn to play it, following a game and imagining we are champions, watching a film and deciding to write a book...as in my case.

Every passion arises from the senses: the sight that follows the different colors mixed together at the same time, the taste for the flavors of life, the hearing that perceives the vibrations, the touch that caresses the palm of the hand and transforms an abstract concept, like "touching the voice" during a song that comes out of the phone audio, in a concrete concept, leaving the sounds on my skin. And time...time to dedicate and plan in detail, giving it meaning and perceiving it subjectively, like a one-way mechanism. Every second becomes the past, the present to be grasped and the future to be planned according to the passion that makes life more beautiful.

I planned my time to be able to see from another perspective the place where Freddie and Queen had spent some of their time, the Duck House. The first time I went to Montreux, seeing it from above, my curiosity had turned into a future project that I didn't think would come true so quickly. That daydream I told you about in the *Montreux* chapter was coming true. Standing out for my organizational skills, I tried to plan a trip to share with other fans, inside the villa, at a rather stormy moment due to the virus. I really wanted there to be seven of us, like the number of the shirt Freddie shows in a photo. I heard 7 was his favorite number, coincidentally the symbol of the concept of solitude and completeness. Seven like musical notes, seven like the colors of the rainbow, seven are the lunar cycles and seven are the deadly sins. Each of us had chosen a different color for the T-shirt with Freddie's face and the words *"Freddie's women"*. It was no coincidence that I chose yellow.

Even taking into account that the period was not the best for travelling, desire took over, defying any obstacle that stood in my way. Anxiety grew due to the fear of a closure between States and regions, but my prayers to recover from Covid were heard. A few missing pieces and the puzzle took shape.

The awaited day of departure arrived between anxiety and uncertainties due to the current situation. Inside my huge suitcase I put this big dream of mine, my expectations, the desire to explore and discover this magical place, and a mixture of emotions that pervaded my body and mind. I already knew the way, I just had to wait to get to Clarens, and as the train approached Switzerland, like the first time, the song that symbolized it increased this fantastic feeling.

My world is spinnin'
And spinnin' and spinnin
It's unbelievable
Sends me reeling
Am I dreaming?

A Winter's Tale (Queen, 1995)

I was dreaming again, but this time big. Fate wanted me to open the mailbox to get the keys. I was shaking and laughing at the same time. My autumn story began with the opening of that wooden gate, and as I turned the key, in disbelief, I felt lucky and privileged. It was one of those afternoons in which the days shorten and the little light of the day mingles with the darkness that begins to dominate. How many times had I imagined going down those stairs? I lingered for a few minutes before going inside the house to admire the purple horizon, the flaming yellow and the fairy-tale panorama, just like on the cover of *Made In Heaven*. It was like going into Wonderland, and I felt a bit like Alice in search of an adventure called Duck House, only that here there weren't rabbits to follow, but ducks, lots of ducks everywhere, of different materials and sizes, 106 to be exact, and there were also the real ones outside swimming in peace. Time stopped and emotions came out with a cascade of tears that made me slide to the lakeside.

It was cold in the evening, but the butterflies were safe inside my stomach. I was surrounded by secular trees that blocked the brightness of the moon in the evening, making the environment dark, so I decided to light many candles that spelled his name, Freddie, and a real heart to light up the background, accompanied by the *Ghost Track*, which started while I was trying to start *Mother Love*...

My dreams are all the company I keep

A thin rain started pattering on my face, but it couldn't put out those little flames in in front of me, because your name, Freddie, gave a power to the fire, which apart from the weakness of someone who extinguished in the intact wax, the others continued to shine, leaving my smile among the dense branches. That was my center of the earth, and that was where I wanted to be.

> *Now I'm here*
> *With the rain running down my face*
> *Your matches still light up the sky*
> *And many a tear lives on in my eye*
>
> *Now I'm Here* (Queen, 1975)

I headed for the house. I entered on tiptoe, slowly, so as to be able to carefully observe the interior furnishings that brought us back to the 70s, making me feel tiny in front of this important accomodation. The soft lights made the atmosphere even warmer. I admired each piece of furniture and ornaments combined with taste. I observed in detail thinking that you, Freddie, had seen each object too, and through your eyes I imagined how much fun you were having in there, because that was just the place to relax and get inspired after a tiring day of recording in the Studios. In there, time seemed to have stopped.

A chat around the fireplace and an impromptu dance, with the base of *I Want To Break Free,* with a vacuum cleaner found there by chance, a few laughs and I headed towards the "Queen of Hearts" room. It was all so surreal. I got into bed and stared at the ceiling thinking that you used to do the same too, Freddie, when you weren't sleepy, and through the crack that was created between the two curtains I realized that the rain had stopped, but the candles still lit up the atmosphere and under the reflection of the stars one could glimpse the wooden house facing the lake.

It was really crazy.

Just like Alice I woke up in the backyard next to my roommate. It was now time for tea, black with a little milk like you used to have, Freddie. We started sipping it under the roof of the wooden house built almost on the lake, looking at the photos you had taken in that garden. It seemed like a spring day and the sun warmed our newfound souls.

Dressed like Freddie before being accompanied on the grand tour of Montreux, we took pictures in the same places, appreciating the exceptional possibility that we had strongly desired. After that we went to greet him in person in the square where Freddie was always waiting for us with that fist raised, in what had become a greeting that we exchanged with nostalgia. That moment of hugs around him became so intimate and affectionate that we didn't want to leave anymore. Upon arrival tears were inevitable and as time went on, we began to admire him from head to toe with love. The attempt to put a necklace with two dangling hearts around his neck as a memento was in vain, because while I was jumping to get to put it on, it suddenly fell to the ground and broke, causing me to find the two hearts in my fist again. I put them in my coat pocket and surrounded the microphone with the chain left over from my necklace. We sang *Love of My Life* out loud, in front of the smiles of passers-by who stopped to take pictures of us. Personally I had chosen to wear the king's cape and crown and the others had chosen the outfit of various video clips. One girl was dressed 70s, two others like in live and yet another had chosen *Living on My Own*, while Divina represented him in *Crazy Little Thing Called Love*, dressed in leather from head to toe and with white knee pads.

We said goodbye to Freddie but it was just a hello, because we would be back after seeing all the Queen places with other people and the tour guide, who kindly explained and informed us about everything that happened in the years in which Queen visited Montreux. This time I had the opportunity to go deeper into what was happening, the events of the time and the places they frequented. I saw Freddie's Japanese kimono framed up close inside the Hotel Palace Montreux, and I didn't miss the opportunity to take a picture. It was so large that it enveloped you, but it fitted you so well that you looked like a God.

We continued the tour seeing other places such as the concert halls, the pub the band frequented, the studio where the recordings took place, but what struck me was the road along the lake that Freddie sometimes made on foot from the hotel to the recording studio, incredulous that the locals wouldn't stop him, and consequently thinking he wasn't recognized. But it wasn't like that. The Swiss were so respectful and discreet that they gave him the space he needed. Perhaps one of the many reasons why Freddie liked Montreux.

In that road, the assorted and bright colors of the flowers and trees form the backdrop to the lake, making it even more evocative. And to make this journey even more memorable, we toasted under the statue of Freddie and spent a few hours in his company before returning to the Duck House.

Inside the house your beautiful voice came powerfully from the stereo, but it was as if you were there among us. It had such a timely effect that I couldn't help but imagine you sitting in that yellow armchair and laughing while you played Scrabble. It was stronger than me imagining you in every corner of that house and wondering if you had ever counted all the ducks as I did, since you nicknamed it The Duck House, or if you had touched where I was touching and saw what I was seeing. If this is a dream, don't wake me up!

After a very few hours of sleep, on the other hand, I got up very early with my heart pounding because it was time to get back to reality. Time had passed so quickly that I didn't realize the days that had passed. I left a thought inside the notebook that I found on the top shelf of the library: *"Sorry I wasn't listening, I was thinking about Freddie Mercury"*. I went to the dining room for the last breakfast and by magic, on the brick-coloured floor, I found clearly visible a white thread which had turned into the infinity sign: for me it meant the emphasis of a lifelong bond, and of a boundless emotion. The confirmation that the verb to love would remain in the infinitive. It reminded me of the time I found a pound under the rug despite the fact that I had never been to London…How many coincidences!

I went out to breathe deeply the clean air, holding back the emotion. The light blue color of the lake conveyed even more the peace that was perceived in Montreux, and the dry leaves that crunched under my feet, together with the singing of the birds, were the only sounds that consoled me.

Down gave way to aurora and sunrise, finding me on the bench near the lake where I felt immersed in nature, where the fairy tale had begun, aided by the same panorama that enchanted with its monochromatic color. The lake and the mountains seemed to be one. At that moment I wished I had the superpowers to stop time, but unexpectedly they gave us a few more hours. We took advantage of it for a last farewell to the bronze Freddie. In those four days I had looked out over the lake several times, waiting to see a swan without success, thinking that in winter they would migrate to warmer places. Instead it was a surprise to see two swans swimming right in front of the statue. One of the fans nicknamed them Freddie and Jim. She said "Freddie!" and the swan came towards us, while the other one moved away on the opposite side. It stayed with us for a while, after which we both said goodbye, because it was time to go back to get our bags.

As soon as I got off in the Duck House garden, I went up to the wooden house to take a last look at the wonderful panorama from there. Like the diamond heart of the ocean, I touched the hearts forgotten in my coat pocket since that first night, when I'd tried to put the necklace around his neck. I wanted to leave him something of myself in the belief that Freddie was right there, in that immense lake, so I threw them into the cold water that morning, following their fall to the bottom with my eyes. I stood motionless for a few moments, and as I turned to go down the stairs, I saw the swan arrive silently.

It was a sign, not a coincidence. I called out to it loud enough to drive the other girls out of the house: "Freddie!" and it continued to swim elegantly approaching the wooden house. It had found its way to its Duck House. I ran into the house to bring it something to eat and served it like a treasure hunt, one piece after another, until I got it out of the water. Surprisingly it got closer and even let itself be fed. A more beautiful ending could not exist. A sign from above.

I had emptied my suitcase of dreams and filled it with your experience in Montreux, with your music inspired by this enchanted place, and with the wind from the lake that would have transported me to another place where you were born and raised, in the country of which you felt like a citizen and where you gave the maximum of your genius. I wore your shadow as protection and I took you away with me, forever, just like Leonardo da Vinci did with his Mona Lisa, and your gaze, just like his, accompanied mine.

So this exceptional experience taught me that only by persevering, the impossible becomes possible, goals become achievable and dreams come true. Dreams lead the way to our well-being and following them is the way to reach seventh heaven.

***

When asked *"Are you fan of Freddie if...?"* I could not answer otherwise:

"If I came to live you, inside the Duck House".

Instead, the other fans responded like this:

"If you can't resist answering... EEEEEEEEEOOOOOO."

"If you still get goosebumps when you hear him sing."

"If when you think of him and hear him sing, tears come down and you can't help it."

"When children shout: Mamaaa» and you answer "Just killed a man»."

"If you cry listening to his songs."

"If as soon as you hear a few notes of one of his songs on TV, you leap from your chair and start singing it too."

"If I listen to a song and then I say: one more and that's it. Even though I know it's not true."

"I can't do without him, his voice, his music. It's in my life and in my heart".

"If hearing his voice you get excited every time as if it were the first. If you cry without even realizing the tears are coming down. Freddie I still love you forever and ever."

"If you always look at him as if he's one of the coolest things you've ever seen in your life, Freddie has the catch-all charisma!"

"If when you hear Radio Gaga you start dancing like him on stage at Live Aid."

"If when they broadcast an advertisement with one of his songs you don't change the channel. If you don't answer the phone to keep hearing the ringtone, Don't Stop Me Now.*"*

"If you are sad and suddenly hearing his voice your eyes light up and your heart has extrasystoles."

"If you like every song, singing with that amazing voice."

"If you've been recognized on social media for being the most active fan of the week."

"If you get emotional every time you hear him"

"If, in addition to all that you have said, when you turn off the stereo in the car you tell him: «Sorry, but I have to go»."

"If...when you hear his songs you start dancing like crazy."

"If, in hearing him sing, you get emotional and a few notes are enough to understand that it is a song in which he gives us his voice."

I'm coming home to my sweet mother love
Mother Love (Queen, 1995)

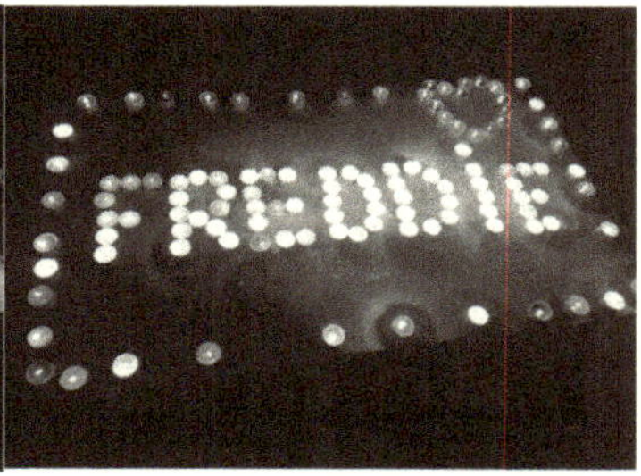
FREDDIE

Sorry
I Wasn't Listening
I Was
Thinking About
FREDDIE
MERCURY

LONDON

"Later I attended the Ealing Art School, in London…While the passion for music was absorbing me more and more, also at that time, Roger and I had a stall at Kensington Market. Our goal was to get to the top."
Freddie Mercury – A life in his words

November 24, 2021 was not a Sunday like that cursed November 24, 1991, but a Wednesday, the day when I felt strongly compelled to find myself for the first time in front of Freddie's house in Garden Lodge, to pay him homage and thank him once again. Nothing or anyone would have stopped me, neither the accident I had a few minutes before leaving nor the restrictions of the British government. My car journey to the Rome airport began the day before the anniversary of Freddie's death, seemingly alone but in the company of his singing voice *Doing All Right,* a line of which, *"Where will I be this time tomorrow?",* seemed to expect an answer from me.

"I'll be with you" I spontaneously answered, without hiding my tension for the long journey, with a car that had just had an accident, even if for him I would have gone to the end of the world. But I was fine, someone had protected me. For the first time I was going to the country that had adopted him, where he had spent his youth, and where his creativity had soared. In London, in the place where he felt free. I was driving thinking that by traveling so many chilometers I could listen to all the songs without interruptions, and think about everything that was happening to me, how much I had dedicated myself to Freddie and Queen these past few years, and how much they had filled my life with beauty.

The next morning my dream trip had just taken off on a plane to this cosmopolitan capital. Somebody says that those who leave us are on their way to heaven, and they help us from up there by sending signs. It's really true. Some started when we were flying over Montreux, which seemed so small, surrounded by clouds that covered the rest of the lake. Seeing him was heart-pounding as usual, but this time I was in the city that had given Freddie the opportunity to grow as an artist, to exhibit in different places which I would have liked to see one by one, even though I knew it was impossible, in such a short time. Here I met other fan friends. I was happy at the thought of what I would see, because in London there are so many places where Queen played at the beginning, the places they frequented, or the houses where Freddie had lived before buying the house of his dreams, and that was exactly where I wanted to go right away.

The gray and cloudy weather represented our state of mind in remembering that sad day of thirty years ago. We quickened our steps towards his house. It is incredible how, within a few meters, you pass from a deafening street crowded with traffic, to Logan Place, where silence reigns, right there where Garden Lodge is located. My steps slowed down at the sight of that door that I had seen many times in photos and that now was in front of me. I opened my arms and put my ear to catch even the smallest noise, but the silence was unreal. In the meantime, I joined some fans who had approached the sidewalk in front of his house wanting to see more, but the high walls blocked the view. I moved to the side where, through some sturdy, bare branches, I saw the window of Freddie's bedroom. I almost thought that at any moment he would appear behind that slightly moved curtain...My skin was crawling. I imagined him there, looking out to enjoy his garden. If that tree could talk, every leaf of it would tell of happy days, when he organized his parties and invited friends to lunch or dinner, and he personally also took care of the menu, because he wanted everything to always be perfect and please others, after all altruism was part of him.

He would tell of the day he started planting in the garden and impatiently threw down his tools, because he had only come into this world to create masterpieces in music, of the time he went to see if his koi carp were doing well, of the time he called his cat and worried about he absence of one of them; it would tell of his healthy laughter, but also of the days of his illness. I don't want to label them as sad days, but as days of an awareness of a life lived to the fullest with that energy that was not dying out, but only transforming.

I was there, but I couldn't be satisfied with seeing only part of the roof of his beloved home. I always find a way to get what I want, even if it means going against everyone. That day, I put the lightness and longing of my traveling companions under my wings, and together we flew to better see Freddie's garden of wonders. We found a way to do it. And though dry leaves littered the streets of London, this paradise was clean and tidy: the trees pruned, as he would have liked. Behind the house, between the outside wall and the kitchen, a small tree with yellow leaves was sticking out, and above its roots, spread out over the floor, was a kind of mosaic with four white corners and a small dark gray sculpture in the center, bonsai style, a parasol and blue chairs. Sloping chairs leaned against the marble table, as if they were waiting for someone to straighten them after the rain to sit down and spend an afternoon in the open air. Contained in that corner, the cherry tree totally devoid of leaves really seems to be in mourning…

I was enchanted and incredulous to see all this "from the height of my expectations", or rather, just like Brian when he performed his guitar from the roof of Buckingham Palace to celebrate Queen Elizabeth's Golden Jubilee, with the only difference that our roof was not so important in everyone's eyes, but it was for that beautiful view it had offered us, Freddie's thriving paradise. Thinking about it, I still get chills and those priceless images still flash in my eyes.

I was amazed that someone was tending the garden as if Freddie were still there. Or maybe he was really there in the guise of the *invisible man*, and I was on his trail, in his head and behind his back with a veil of euphoria spread over the grass." I lowered my wings" and we returned to our feet on the ground again in front of *Garden Lodge* sign, which was difficult to read in the dark, and where many fans from different countries were waiting for us.

It seems that darkness arrives earlier in London, but strangely the sky above his refuge remained shaded gray, as if he wanted us to see his world even at night, which not even the lights would have made so magical. It was his piece of sky, not that of the whole city. It was as if he was still in there and the world had left him out.

"Seeing this house is like opening his heart" Sonia whispered in my ear, demonstrating that she was so satisfied with the great gesture we were making, and she continued: "I love this house, because for me it's pure magic. It was his home, his safety, his world, his peace, as ours is for each of us. That is why when he felt that his time had come, he immediately returned to his beloved Garden Lodge, and for the last few days he wanted to be accompanied to the rooms to see his pictures and his porcelain vases. He was that house, because there he had enclosed his passion, his world."

His words moved me and made me think more. He wanted to carry within himself, at least the images, kept forever. There was his whole world in there, made up of objects that he had chosen with care, but also of feelings, memories, affections and friendship. We were right there, only a high wall separated us from that house, but it didn't prevent us from feeling our emotions, because the air we breathed was the same as beyond those brown bricks. We lit yellow candles next to others and the growing flowers.

From the stero of a car parked in front of the door, at high volume, Freddie's voice was heard singing *It's a Hard Life*.

It's just a simple fact of life
It can happen to anyone
I try to fight back the tears
How it hurts (Yeah) deep inside (Oh, yeah)

It hurt not to see him there and I held back the tears until a fan arrived and knelt down placing on the wall one of Freddie's photos with a dedication, taken during the recording of *Play the Game*, coincidentally my favorite, because in that photo, with that curly black hair, he looks like my father when he was young. I felt the rumble of the beat in my ears. At that moment I wished it would rain to confuse my tears with the drops from the sky. I walked away to privately experience the outburst for Freddie's absence that is felt here a lot, but my dear friend came to get me and her sweet words dried my face. It was almost 6:48, the time of his last earthly breath. We stood in line in front of the Garden Lodge sidewalk for a minute of silence. Someone loudly started the countdown. At the end of the last second they all shouted his name: *"Freddie! Freddie forever, Freddie I love you, love of my life"*, and they began to sing the song of the same name for him.

I wonder if Mary was listening to us. If she had looked out onto the terrace, she would have seen with her own eyes the love we still feel for his eternal love. Maybe a greeting…surely the chorus of fans reached the Mews where policemen who had closed the entrance, after a while joined us for a few minutes. We came in peace, like that three-year-old boy whom his mother approached in front of the candles gleaming in the dark, which he gazed at in amazement. The musice was still in the background and she picked him up and started dancing. The effect that Freddie's voice had on the children was also felt after a few minutes, when two others, a little older, came and left their scooters next to the flower bouquets, one blue and the other pink, and they began to dance. Those kids were amazing. They didn't think about their game, but about the gesture. Having seen that everyone had left something in front of and next to the door, and perhaps they felt compelled to do so too. They had to give something and the only thing they possessed at that moment was their game, and they continued to have fun with the music that lit up their little souls.

The atmosphere filled again with Freddie's powerful voice asking *Who Wants to Live Forever?* We all want to live forever, but not all of us are lucky enough to live a long life. But whether it's long or short, it's the intensity that matters, what you offer to others, what you give without pretending to receive, what you create and remain for years to come, just like Freddie did. We were there exactly after thirty years remembering him and his music, and his Phoebe said: *"People will listen to his songs for a long time. His music gives hope and makes them live."*

Surely those children who will come back to relive these very intense musical emotions in front of their beloved home, perhaps influenced by it, will still listen to it. I'm sure some of them will bring a guitar, with the memory vivid in mind. But for us, forever was our present day, jus as Freddie sang in the last lines of that melancholy song.

I would have stood there for hours, but I had the desire to see other places where Freddie had lived and one of them was very close: Stafford Terrace, his first home. Together with my friends, we preferred to walk despite the cold at the end of November, enjoying the view of the typical houses of a London still in the 70s, the same buildings with lots of bay windows, the same characteristic atmosphere, and this street that used to be remained the same in its tranquility. We arrived at number 12, Freddie's first house. The light coming from a house on the first floor, with the part of the side window without curtains, also illuminated the bery few steps I climbed, leaning out slightly to see only the ceiling. One cannot fail to feel an emotion at the thought that Freddie lived there, and that he had taken his first steps starting from here.

Given the proximity, we headed towards another house where Freddie met with the other Queen, at 36 Sinclair Road. Here we were surprised by what we found in front of the entrance, namely two cardboard boxes with the words *Freddie's Flowers* on them. The idea that someone had sent fresh flowers sounded great to us, but we asked ourselves: "Why here and not at Garden Lodge?". To solve the doubts Sonia sent an e.mail to the distribution company, which kindly replied. Their company was named after Freddie G, a big fan of Freddie Mercury, adding that they had been a sort of treasure hunt. Whether it was all random or not, it seemed like a great coincidence.

But what I wondered most was simply a question any fan would ask: do those who live there know that ideas for those timeless songs were born here? At that moment I absolutely wanted an answer, so much so that I wanted to knock to ask if they knew that Freddie Mercury lived here in the early 70s, and if they could open up this historic place to us fans, but civic sense prevailed over curiosity: I took my hand away from the door and smiled for my envy, leaving even those boxes there without a name to which to be addressed. I must say that I was sorry not to deliver them to their true addressee and while we were returning, I expressed this wish of mine to Sonia who approved, and we remembered the place where we would return as soon as we woke up.

We began to get tired and we decided to continue the evening, just to stay on topic, with the vision of the film *Bohemian Rhapsody*, which Italian TV was broadcasting for the first time. Half of the film we watched on our mobile while having dinner in a pub near Garden Lodge. Here too we surprisingly found photos of Freddie and other singers. "I wonder if he used to come here at the time". How many questions, with uncertain answers that left the desire to know. We finished the second part of the film at the Hotel. Luca was truly fantastic in finding a way for us to see it on TV.

Around four in the morning, the thought of completing the mission that some force majeure had chosen us to carry out, made us jump up. It was just us females and the street cleaning machines. We didn't even feel three degrees above zero, so the adrenaline was high. We hoped they hadn't thrown them away, as they had left them near the sidewalk. In fact, we only found one. Better than nothing. The flowers had resisted the humidity of the night. We were happy like two little girls when they pick flowers and give them to mom. Mission accomplished.

"They came to him in a different way, because it wasn't a delivery, it was a treasure hunt."

"And we have traveled the last stage, as if they were waiting for us" I completed Sonia's thought, who concluded: "We were the last link, the decisive one. The relay team returning to base."

We had chills on our skin, certainly not from the freezing cold. We bowed respectfully, taking a cue from the photo of Freddie, where he is down on one knee, and just as he held the microphone tightly we felt a pang in our hearts. We firmly assumed that Freddie was with us and watching over us.

The next day the clouds had given way to the sun, which led the way towards the house that welcomed him as soon as he arrived in London when he was still a teenager, exactly in Feltham. I was reminded of the few images of Freddie with his college buddies, at one point raising his arms with clenched fists. He was 18 years old. He was happy and full of dreams. Fortunately, moving from Feltham, he settled in London where he met the people who would soon turn out to be the right ones to create a successful band, Brian and Roger and later John too. Together they flew to the moon to aim for the stars.

It seemed to me that young Freddie, with long hair and dressed in white, was walking with us, on that long street where the houses all looked the same, but as we approached, one was different, and we recognized it by the Blue Plaque displayed on the facade, issued by English Heritage: *Freddie Mercury (Fred Bulsara) 1946-1991 Singer and songwriter Lived here.* The open gate invited entry, and still in my imagination he led the way. He entered the small courtyard, turned his head towards us and disappeared behind the white door, while we stood on the side of the road, still believing in this fairy tale. It was so tempting to follow him, but we stopped on the sidewalk, because after a few seconds a man parked his car in front of it and entered as if it were his home, bringing us back to reality. In fact it was his. The current owner looked at us strangely. Maybe he didn't understand that for us fans, the Bulsara surname was carved into every brick. I can't tell if he realized how lucky he had been in buying that tiny but big apartment and that we were there for Freddie, because a part of him was in his room, where he wrote the first lines, which he kept safe under his pillow.

Hello young Bulsara! It was nice to "meet" you at your parents' house.

A short distance away we also found the street dedicated to Freddie. I understood why it was right there when I read a billboard with the words *World Zoroastrian House...* Our journey then continued to another Queen-branded place, the famous Wembley Stadium. *Lads! Do you hear his voice? Our response to his eeeeoooo, was alwayse eeeeeoooo...*

Even though it had changed a lot, the idea that Queen had performed live there made it seem more majestic that it already was, with its height and bright colors. We took pictures as if to pierce the sky with a finger, and continued towards the centre. Unfortunately Richoux, Freddie's favorite restaurant, was closed. We wanted to have lunch there and taste his favorite dish, *welsh rarebit*. It was amazing how so many clues always lead to the band or to Freddie himself. Floors, black and white rhombus or square staircases, terracotta cats, passing by chance to the Ray Ban store, the Hard Rock Cafè where I saw his original microphone and then the shop entirely dedicated to them, *Queen The Greatest* in Carnaby Street, even the gigantic photo of the full band, in the subway, under the photo of Jimi Hendrix and a plaque dedicated to Freddie's idol.

    The time came to reluctantly say goodbye to two of our faithful companions on this trip for Freddie, who in turn seemed to have influenced the idea of doing it in two days, because the day after our return the restrictions were applied again due to Covid. Mine, as well as Francesco's flight, left later, and we took the opportunity to see some places where Queen had given their concerts. So on our way back to Covent Garden, we stopped at the Royal Opera House, one of the most important theaters in the world. It is no coincidence that Freddie decided to sing right here with Montserrat Caballè. At the entrance, some very significant stage costumes for the history of music and theater were on display.

    Immortalizing each building was a must, so much so that I wanted to see many others, but time didn't permit it and we contented ourselves with continuing towards Leicester Square, right where Capital Radio broadcasted *Bohemian Rhapsody* for the first time, in October 1975. I stopped to stare at the writing above, and instantly imagined myself in front of a radio of the time, listening to speaker Kenny Everett says aloud:

"It's 6 minutes of absolute orgy of sound. The song hasn't even been recorded on a disc yet, it's on tape and in about 5 minutes I'll let you listen to it. Once again Capital Radio has won an extraordinary scoop! Freddie gave me that tape and told us to keep going. Ladies and gentlemen, for the first time in this radio world of ours, we present to you the new Queen single righ now!"

Since morning, these names have been repeating in my ears like a catchphrase: *Galileo, Galileo, Figaro... Magnificooooo.* With this last adjective, the song of the century spoke for itself. No one except Freddie ever expected that song would go so high.

With our mind singing without a voice among the crowded streets, we kept walking toward Trident Studios, which was not too far from there. A strange thing happened here. Although we were at the right address, after passing several times to its house number, we could not find it. I've always thought that nothing happens by chance. In the end, the way their relationship was at the beginning of Queen's career, it never inspired me to see it.

We changed course and soon found ourselves in front of the Dominion Theatre. If the statue had still been above the entrance, it would have given a more imposing aspect to this place. Roger had taken it the the garden of his house, so Freddie would have found himself in a large family, the one he had perhaps always wanted to have, having a good laugh as always, with his longtime friend. However, here Freddie had his last performance on April 14, 1988, and coincidentally it was the last place for us to visit on this short trip to London. Surely I would have liked to see many other places, but I will calmly come back to see the rest. I think I visited the most important in just over 24 hours, those that left a mark on my soul, an image in my eyes and a trace in my heart.

You can find out what it left to my friends Sonia by reading her comments:

"Our trip to London was magical. No one will ever understand...no one...Going past Garden and the Mews at 5am. Just us and his house. I'm honored. I still feel that sensation on my skin. Freddie was with us. I have no doubts. He watched over us the whole time. We were the last link, but the decisive one. The relay team returning to base, I have chills on my skin. Garden Lodge is the closest thing to him. I feel his emotions. They are touchable. That photo of that room...it sends them to you. Our trip to London was something of a relic. I will never, ever, ever forget that sky. I think about it every moment, every day. The most exciting thing in the world.
"

***

I come from London town
I'm just an ordinary guy
Lazing on a Sunday Afternoon (Queen, 1975)

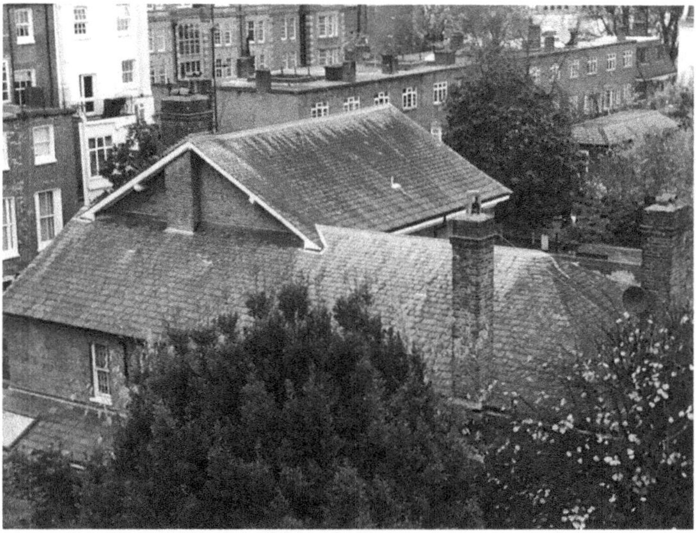

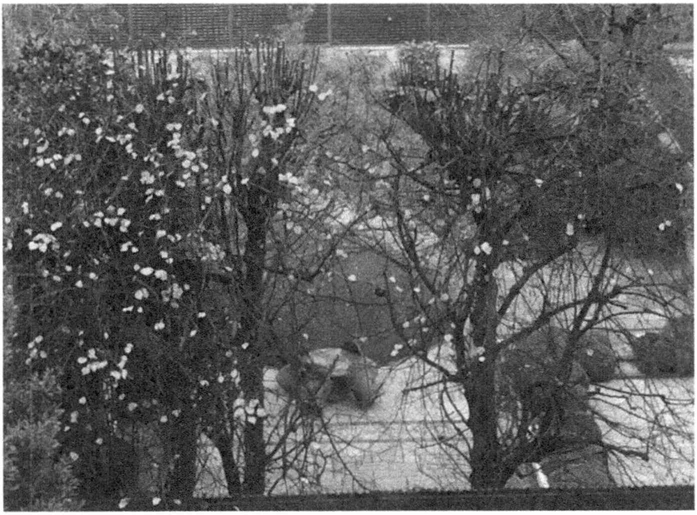

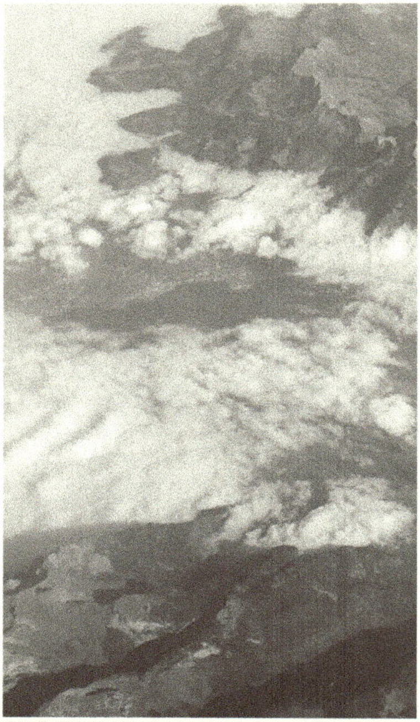

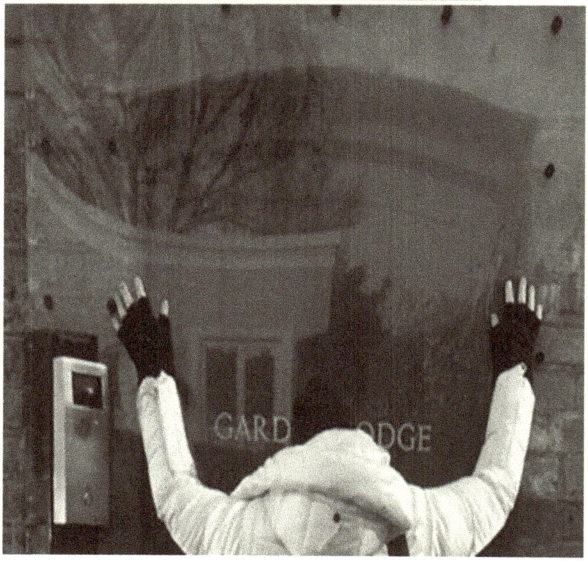
GARD
ODGE

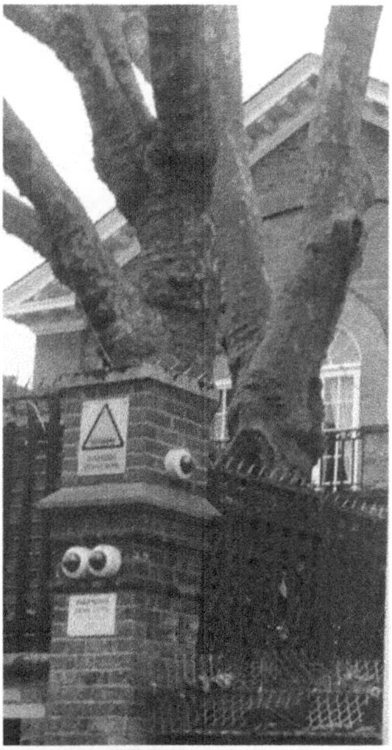

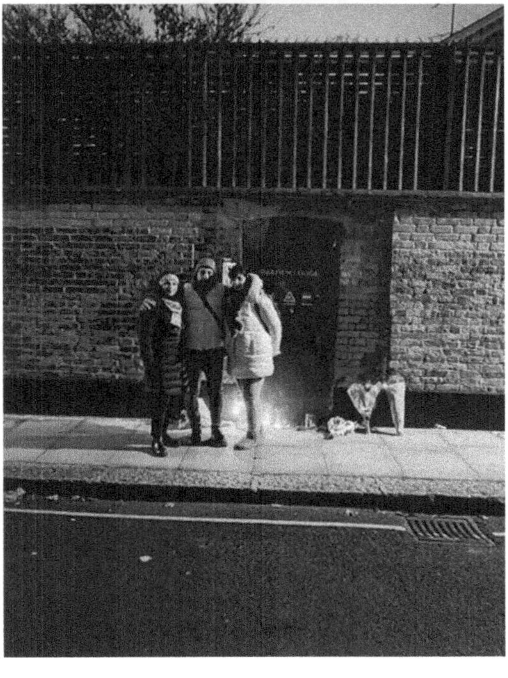

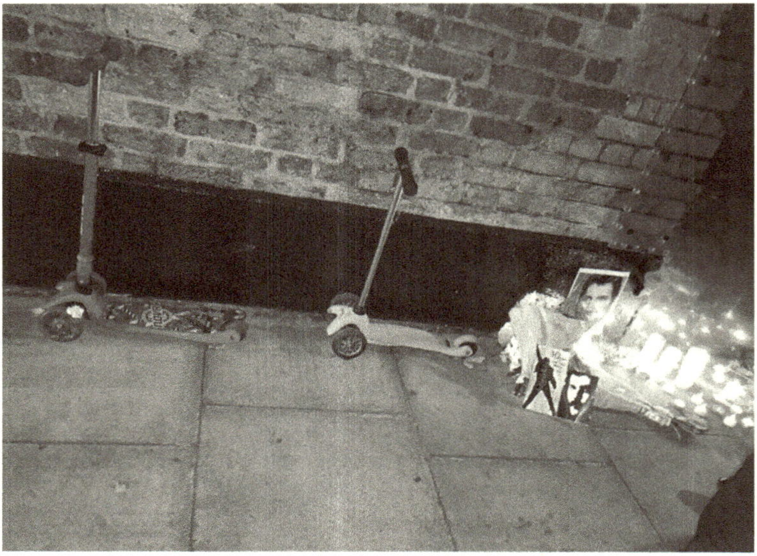

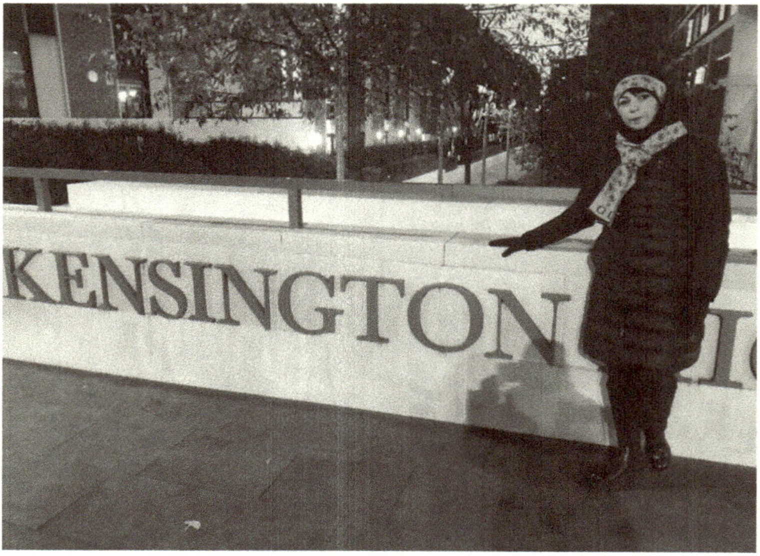
KENSINGTON

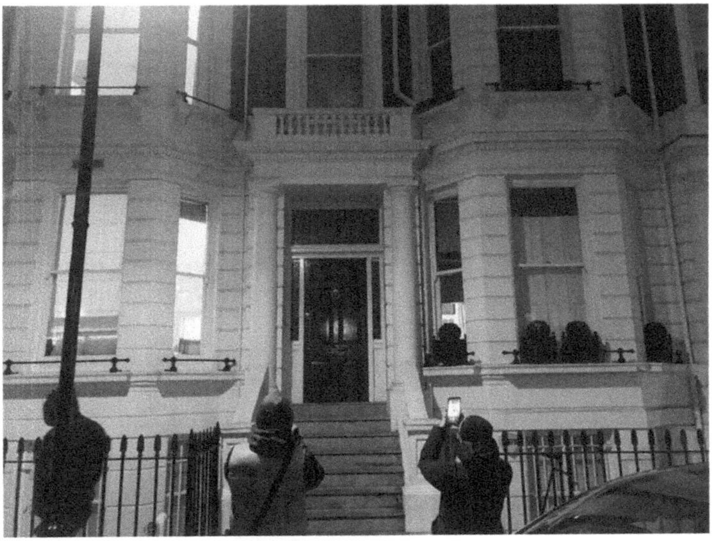

WEMBLEY

DOMINION THEATRE

FREDDIE
MERCURY CLOSE
(PRIVATE ROAD)
RIVATE
CAR
PARK

RESTAURANT
Richoux

AN "UNEXPECTED" MEETING

This is the only life for me, yeah
Surround myself around my own fantasy
Keep Passing the Open Windows (Queen, 1983)

How many times have we fans said "If I could have seen Queen and Freddie at least once", or "How much I wanted to attend that concert", "Too bad, I was small and my parents didn't let me go", or "Who knows what would it have been like to see or meet him?"

I tried to fantasize, to let myself go chasing a dream, a hypothetical encounter, as if it had really happened, experiencing the power of the decision to continue to control reality according to my will, to live an illusion without disappointment, a dream nourished by emotions such as love, hope, gratitude, interest and enjoyment.

For months I have traveled with my mind, and I have daydreamed to tell what had never happened, all the words I wanted to say to Freddie and the desire to let him know what he never knew. My mind flew, going back in time, and with it also my body, which showed the age corresponding to those years. A dive into the past, but with the knowledge of the present. However, the idea of traveling back in time fascinated me so much that I went inside the story and wrote it as if it were true. A kind of science fiction, aided by the only "machines" capable of making me see the past, like a mental "chronovisor", while remaining in the present. Technology has helped me understand the details of events through videos, but the reconstruction of the real events was already all in my head. While writing I felt positive emotions. I threw myself into it headlong, identifying myself to the point of perceiving it as if I had really lived it.

So much so that when it was all over I felt a veil of sadness.

This my real, crazy and pure fantasy, which started listening to the first verses of *These Are the Days of Our Lives*.

Sometimes I get to feelin'
I was back in the old days, long ago
When we were kids, when we were young

***

Monaco di Baviera, 1985

On 1st September, as a reward for my perseverance, I was in Munich for a study holiday. I had insisted so much on this scholarship for a very good reason. Three days later, through friends, we received an invitation card for the long-awaited birthday party, in which it was written exactly this:

"*Freddie Mercury*
Invites you to
A Black and White Drag Ball
For his birthday of
Hendersons
Thursday 5 September 1985 - From 10 pm - 4 am
Please come in Black/White Drag Costume - Entrance by invitation only - Hendersons, Munich"

Personally, I was very enthusiastic about the idea of something that I wanted to do at all costs. I had done everything to participate and I had succeeded. It was a themed birthday, so to keep up with the others, we immediately started preparing both the clothes and the gifts. I could not have had a better opportunity than this to implement my plan. On the evening of Thursday, September 5, we walked to Henderson's Night Club, one of the best clubs in this city.

People arrived with the most bizarre means and the four of us (me, Sonia, Luca and Frank) were certainly no less, belting out *I Want to Break Free* and pedaling on a rickshaw painted with a piano keyboard. The euphoria of almost adults and the desire to have fun were through the roof. As soon as I got out, my eyes were on a man with long, curly hair wearing a witch's hat.

"Brian May?" I widened my eyes. "Queen's guitarist?"

As he entered, I stopped at the entrance curious to observe the decorations, when Sonia took my hand and catapulted me inside, with the liveliness that characterized her.

The swarming of people and the *cheers* of the toasts did not dominate the musical notes of *New York*, which at full volume accompanied the other people who arrived, rigorously dressed and accessorized in black and white: checks, rhombuses, stripes, polka dots...even the glasses and dessert bowls were in these contrasting colours. The floor, the hanging flowers, the armchairs and the ceiling also formed a two-tone frame.

I was literally dragged by my older friends, who used to go to parties. I knew the rule was: men dressed as women, and women dressed as a famous male character, but I didn't do it because the character in question was the birthday boy. So, just to stay on topic, I wore the only dress of these two colors that I had on hand, the black college uniform with the white collar, just like in the dream previously told, and the matching backpack in horizontal stripes, where I put something from the future, useful for my return to the past.

My shyness made me feel out of place among so many people, some of whom dressed very extravagantly. It has always been like this: at the beginning I observe, I study the environment and the people, then slowly, when I gain confidence, I begin to integrate. At the sight of those black and white checkered sofas, I was reminded of the long afternoons at my grandmother's house, when, to satisfy my childhood curiosity, I watched my uncle and his companions commit themselves for entire minutes to move the pieces. I sat down feeling like I was inside a chessboard, waiting to see the White Queen in her center square.

My friends disappeared from time to time and returned with a glass in hand, finding me punctually motionless in my place. The more I looked around, the more I seemed to be inside a crazy dream: half-naked men, brides, hostesses, strange hats, women with cat make-up, and even a stuffed panda and a zebra, wearing the same nuances that represented the black and white world of animals.

I noticed him, surrounded by four men, watching the zebra together with Barbara Valentin, with a smile that didn't go unnoticed. He had on a military army general's jacket with important epaulettes, ropes, hanging medals, his beloved Adidas Samba and argyle tights, obviously black and white. An unusual combination, but one that looked great on him. The only man who looked even more macho with the eye pencil on.

"Here's Freddie!" my friend said to me raising her voice, since the noise didn't allow me to hear well up close.

I looked at him like a lover at first crush with all the naivety of my years and I answered her almost stammering: "He's really…really nice…". Since I had entered I had followed his every move without taking my eyes off him.

A moment before he was in front of us, a moment later I saw him with the floreal crown that the actress Jane Seymour wore on her head, during the show she had done with Freddie, dressed as a bride in Fashion Aid.

There was a specific reason why I had tried to be at the 39th birthday party of the great lead singer of Queen, Freddie Mercury, to which almost 400 people were invited. I had been transported into the past, from one era to another, where reality and fantasy interwined, making me feel in the balance. It was as if I was living in the present having completely projected myself into the past. I don't know if I could have resisted not revealing everything that had happened after 1985. I was afraid of involuntarily saying too much. Part of me wanted to relate the events that had transpired, and the other part wanted to be silent. They would have thought I was crazy and wouldn't have believed me. So paying attention to what I said was the first rule I imposed on myself, even if it wasn't that easy, because the sense of duty was too strong.

And as the two thoughts clashed in my mind, I saw Freddie jump into the arms of a man dressed in blue who, along with another one dressed in red, was among the few to break the rule of colors. Later he continued to meet other people present. I recognized the lead singer of Culture Club, Boy George, who in those years sang that song called *Karma Chameleon*, the lyrics of which could not have been more apt for the situation I was living in. I began to sing softly and move to the catchy rhythm in perfect Motown style:

Come and go
It should be easy to love
If your colors were like my dreams

Under the *mirror ball* typical of the 80s, Freddie spoke to a girl with two tails and the face full of false freckles, wearing a white shirt, a fine black tie with stripes and a light beige hat circled by a black ribbon.

"It's his ex-girlfriend, Mary Austin, his great friend now, and that shirtless over there in a black bow tie and all wet in champagne is Jim, his current boyfriend", a familiar voice reported to me.

"Yes, I recognize her", I replied without looking away. I adored Mary for her character and for remaining a point of reference to Freddie. I looked at her with admiration and wanted to introduce myself, but the thought of being intrusive prevented me. As for Jim, I already knew everything about him. I had brought his book *My years with Freddy Mercury*, which I was finishing reading. Later, Freddie posed for photographers. He stared into the camera lens with such a sensual gaze that his sex appeal could be perceived even from a distance. After taking a picture with John Reid, he took off his jacket to be photographed with Brian May, and in his suspenders you could see the cartridges full of lead, which indicated that being outrageous was part of him. The cameras continued to shoot and the photographic shots immortalized Freddie at the top of his physical shape.

The time for greetings has come. A gigantic cake in the shape of a grand piano, and another three-tier with his portrait, were surrounded at the edges by black and white candles, on which Freddie blew out just two. He did it with Jim Hutton beside him and with the help of Peter Freestone in a gypsy costume. To his left was his manager, Paul Prenter, who was breathing down his neck the entire time. The usual friends, David Wigg, in a cassock, Joe Flanelli, Peter Strake and even Richard Young, the band's photographer, were always around him. Also present was Jim Beach, Queen's manager/lawyer. Among the applause, all those present whished him a *Happy Birthday*. He was standing right next to us, when suddenly he turned around and said:

"My dears, a little more champagne?"

His voice was a little dull and his gaze a little lost. Immediately instinctively I approached him to ask in a low voice: "Are you okay?"

A few minutes earlier I had seen from behind someone scurrying off after I had handed him a glass. Freddie turned at me with a slightly absent air, gave a small smile, but didn't answer. Besides, who was I to ask him if he was okay?

Everyone had glasses in hand except me. I almost never drink and in the crowds I didn't want to drink because I didn't like losing control and even more on this occasion I mustn't lose my temper when I heard Freddie's delicate voice:

"A glass for this little girl" he said looking at me as if to answer my previous question. "I'm fine. Come one, let's all make a toast together."

"Um, thanks, but I don't drink, because…" I answered halfway, unable to find the right excuse because I didn't expect this invitation from Freddie, and embarrassment was immediately perceived in my voice. He stared at me smiling an made one of his jokes:

"Here it's forbidden not to drink, *darling*". He took his glass and raised it, addressing everyone present, almost losing his balance. I realized he wasn't well.

"It's Louise Roederer's Cristal" Paul intervened, in a sugary voice, without taking his eyes off him, as it to confirm. "Freddie's favorite. Trying is believing, and if you really don't like it, the catering has brought Evian water", he added, shifting his gaze to me and laughing. I looked younger than my age and maybe that's why I felt a bit teased by the latter. I instantly connected Prenter's simple dress, T.shirt and dark trousers, with the man I'd seen handing the glass to Freddie and saying something in his ear. A doubt arose…

Freddie came closer and asked me *"What's your name?"*, just like that April 12, '78, during the Europen *News Of The World Tour* in Svezia, when during the introduction of *It's Late* he asked someone in the audience. And since he didn't hear any names, he answered himself *"I think she said Sandra or something"*, as if he had to answer someone close to him. He did the same with me, but instead of Sandra he said Ruby, perhaps because my face had turned fiery red, and I wasn't answering him from shame.

"Let's say similar…*My name is Rudina*, in my part they say Rudi for friends "I replied with a slightly funny facial mimicry.

"Oh dear, this diminutive is not new to me", he said wryly. "I know a few people with that name" but he didn't bother to mention who they were.

I knew who he was referring to: Rudi Dolezal, director of several Queen video clips, Rudy Nurejev, the Russian dancer, and his favorite Jamaican painter with brightly colored works, Rudi Patterson.

While the service attendants were cutting the cake, Freddie turned sarcastically towards me, then looking me up and down in my school uniform he added: "Oh, I see you are straight from the school" and laughed putting hand in front of my mouth, eyes fixed on my backpack.

"Of course, inside is the civic education book, in case someone wants to study" I too replied with a joke because I was a bit disappointed, and after this question and answer, to show myself older, I decided to do like them. At that moment pride took over. I climbed onto a chair and took a goblet of champagne, which I raised in a toast and downed it all in one gulp, holding the piece of cake in the other hand, which almost fell over.

"Just another! Just another!" shrieked the voiced around us. "One more drop!". People were screaming, laughing and dancing like crazy. They enjoyed themselves exaggeratedly. After having downed two more glasses, I felt happier and more enterprising, to the point of approaching the birthday boy and saying in a voice that no longer sounded like mine:

"Anyway, with its black and white colors, your cat Miko would have been matching here tonight."

Freddie gave me a weird look and replied: "Honey, none of my cats have that name."

My voice was getting slower and slower. When I perceived that he was not understanding, in the conditions in which I had reduced myself, I tried to remember the year in which he had adopted it, then I realized that it had happened a few years later, and immediately grasping the situation I told him:

"Um, I meant my cat...its name is Miko. I'm not English and sometimes I confuse adjectives "I justified myself instantly.

He said he had two cats named Tom and Jerry, and as he joined his men I found I couldn't keep my eyes focused; despite this inconvenience, after having exchanged a few words, when I saw that he was feeling a little better again, despite my mental confusion, I started looking for the man who had given him a drink. The future memory selected a piece of news that I already knew, but which due to the distraction and the state I was in, had not occured to me at the right time. Inside the glass was some kind of drug cocktail. Or so I had read somewhere. Trying to make room for myself in that jungle of people, I collided with my friend Sonia.

"Where are you going so hurry?" she asked me.

I took her hand and said:

"You have to help me!". I explained the whole situation and in no time we were coalesced like never before. My shyness turned into courage when it came to defending the people I cared about. I was good and dear, as they say, but when it came to championing justice I was always on the front line. I was for the free management of one's life. Everyone had the right to do what they thought was right for them and no one should get in the way.

Strangely, we found him away from Freddie, who was checking the progress of the party. We surrounded him one to the right and the other to the left, looking at him with contempt and asking him precise questions to better understand.

"Can you tell us what was in that glass you gave to Freddie? Otherwise we call the police and tell Freddie directly" I said in a not very fluent English.

"I do not understand" he answered falsely.

"I won't let the black pawn eat the Queen" I told him, convinced I knew the moves of the chess pieces, as he looked at me in surprise.

He started to defend himself, denying his actions, then gave me a shove and walked away getting lost in the crowd. I fell to the ground. I don't know if it's me looking for trouble or if it's trouble finding me, but I regularly find myself involved in difficult situations.

A bouncer came over to figure out what was going on, while Sonia helped me up. After listening to us, he went in his direction. I felt a little lost, with my head so heavy that I didn't understand what was happening to me. It seemed that everyone was hoveing around me. It was as if I was passing out and I lay down on the first sofa I could find, but the confusion stunned me more. I tried to get up again, but my legs wouldn't hold up. At that point I felt arms squeezing me, and in a few moments they dragged me out. Being almost teetotal, I had overstepped the line a bit with a few more glasses. They drove me home and I slept until the constantly ringing phone made me jump up. I picked up the phone and a serious and rather determined man's voice asked me:

"Miss Rubina?"

"Rudina, not Rubina". Yet another who confused the b with the d. "Yes, it's me" I added nervously and half asleep.

"We have the rucksack you forgot last night at the party. You can come and pick it up at the Musicland Studio, which is located in the basement of the Arabella Haus building, in the Bogenhausen district. The sooner the better…"

"I live in the Glockenbachbierte district. It takes me half an hour to get there" I said.

"What a coincidence! Our Hotel is also located in that heighborhood, but I'd prefer that you come and pick it up here" he answered in a firm tone.

All this rush to see me made me think. It was four o'clock in the afternoon. I called a taxi, which arrived within minutes, and set off for the studios. I was a little nervous and asked myself a thousand questions. Who knows if they had seen what was inside the bakpack. And if the cell pone had drang, they would have wondered where this technological device came from and what was inside that thin and modern box. On the display I had a photo of Queen with the children in *The Miracle* (year 1989), then I had a keyring hanging from the pocket of my bakpack which I had turned over an put inside, so that non one would see it. Cabbage! All of this happened a few years later. I began to find possible justifications for the case.

"I'm in trouble" I thought, speeding up as soon as I got out of the taxi. How many clues could they have to doubt that I was hiding something? Being returned to the past perhaps had a price to pay.

Anxiety had made my breathing more labored before I entered, and as I descended the stairs inside, one hand on the silver-colored doorknob to keep my balance, I prayed that I would take it easy. Several paintings with vinyl records hung on the midnight blue walls which made the place darker, but as soon as I turned left everything was clearer and brighter. I saw Queen guitarist Brian May playing pinball. I passed by him without greeting so as not to disturb him and he, who was from behind, didn't even turn his head, he was so concentrated on moving the two cranks so as not to let the ball enter the hole. That machine reminded me of the *Harlem Globetrotters*, the miniature basketball game my parents had given me for New Year's, that I would spend hours and hours playing with when I was just starting to play basketball.

I went straight on and entered a fairly large room where I saw on the left the bassist John Deacon who was reading a newspaper with one leg on the back of a sofa. In front of him the drummer Roger Taylor did the same. To my right, Freddie, dressed in striped shorts and a white tank top, sat on a white L-shaped bench. He was smoking a cigarette in one hand, while leafing through a newspaper with the other. It was strange but pleasant to see people reading instead of using cell phones, as is the custom now.

Almost at the corner of the table I saw my backpack. I stopped in front of him.

"*Hello darling!* They told me that you felt ill last night. I see you've recovered."

"Oh yes! Today I feel better. Thanks". I would have told him the truth about my mission if it hadn't been the second day we exchanged a few words.

"I wanted to tell you that when they delivered the backpack, Jim noticed that there was a statue on the keychain attached to the pocket". He took it off the table and looked at it carefully.

"My God!" he exclaimed. "It's me with my arm raised. I didn't know that someone had dedicated a statue to me. It's a joke, I hope" and he started laughing, even if I noticed a little curiosity in his voice. Then he put it down without looking away.

"Yup...I mean...I don't think it's you. Someone trying to imitate you, maybe...I bought it at a flea market" I replied in a not convincing enough way, but the truth was that I had bought it in a shop called Bazar and located in the main street of Montreux.

Avoiding looking at him in the eyes, I pretended to look for a handkerchief in my trouser pockets and literally changed the subject by saying:

"I didn't have so much fun last night, I have the impression that you didn't either. I don't think all those people were your friends. It all seemed a bit exaggerated to me. Sometimes you seemed lost, or maybe it was just me. Excuse me for telling you, but I also learned that some objects have been broken and some gifts have disappeared."

"Oh darling! Forget it. They're not friends, they're distractions, I don't mind. The party had been organized by Paul and the others. I didn't know everyone, but they know me, that's why they were there" he laughed.

I changed the subject: "Anyway, I wanted to tell you that you're my favorite singer, or rather my idol. I already wanted to tell you yesterday evening" I said as I rubbed my hands out of control. "I saw Live Aid two months ago on TV. You were amazing, fantastic, and Queen were the best band. I liked all the songs you chose for that benefic concert. But what made the difference is *Is This the World We Created*, which you composed exactly one year ago in this studio. The symbol of the event to fight hunger in the world. I wanted to congratulate you."

"Oh! With that concert we did something concrete that helped people watch, listen and donate. If there are people dying of hunger, that's everyone's problem. Sometimes I feel helpless and that was an opportunity to do my part."

I felt embarrassed for having stolen some time from him and for having talked so much, but I continued anyway: "Besides those songs I would have loved to listen to others too, from your solo album or some duets, for example... *Barcelona*."

"*Barcelona*?" he asked with a curiosity that I didn't immediately catch, so I continued:

"Yes, the one for the Olympics, with Montsy..."

As soon as I said the diminutive given by Freddie to Monserrat, I immediately made up for it with a shaking voice, because I realized that the song had come out three years later. It was difficult to instantly calculate even those next few years from the current one. Findind myself in front of him, I was confused for a moment. I had just slipped again into an unforgivable mistake.

He looked at me as if to say: "Darling! What are you saying?"

"That is, I meant…I like the city of Barcelona, and I know that in 1992 the Olympics will be held there…Here. I wanted to tell you this. I knew you like it too. Sorry, my English leaves something to be desired" I remedied, trying to change the subject, without giving him time to answer.

Freddie raised his eyebrows and from his look he seemed to think: "What does this have to do with the concert? But then why are you talking about Barcelona?". "How do you know I like this city?" He said. "Do you already know where the Olympics will take place seven years before?". This speech didn't add up to him, and he looked at me amazed.

I felt so uncomfortable that I blurted out a lot of words in one second:

"But now I have to go because I have a thousand things to do, you know I study here in Munich. Thank you! I hope to see you again" I concluded, leaving him perplexed.

"Darling, you can come back anytime, we're here until November to record songs," he replied, as if he didn't care what he'd heard.

After a *"Thank you"*, I grabbed my backpack and hurried out running up the stairs, two steps at a time. I felt a heat on my face, certainly not due to the heat outside. Involuntarily, I had mentioned things that had happened years later and the invitation to return had certainly not been to please me, but to suspect what was behind it, or so I thought.

I hurriedly jumped the last three stairs outside. I was breathing hard and my legs went on their own. I should have kept what I knew a secret, and avoided casting doubt on myself. Damn me! I always make disasters. I hurried toward the house, terrified of being discovered. I went to bed and put my head under the blanket, as I always did before sleeping, when Frank whispered in my ear: *"Hey! Is everything all right"?*

"Yes, yes, everything is fine". I heaved a sigh. "Actually not". I was shaken and felt the need to tell him everything that had happened. He listened to me and reminded me that we were there to study and have some fun, and that I shouldn't think about it anymore. Frank could not understand that at that moment my internal war was whether to be indifferent or to complete a mission in the name of all the fans. Freddie had a right to know what was to happen in the years to come. The events dedicated to him, but above all I wanted to tell him that he is and will always be among us and that the boundless love of his fans, who remember him every day, has no boundaries.

As this became my constant thought, Frank interrupted me:

"I know a good pastry shop nearby, let's all go eat Käsekuchen with blueberries" he continued without trying to fully understand my perplexity.

We spent a rather carefree afternoon laughing and joking, when I heard my cell phone ring. The only means that connected me to the future, to 2021, was the iPhone, which I tried to use only when needed and secretly.

Having been "transported" back almost 35 years, I was struck by the simplicity of real relationships, the interactions of a time that I had somewhat forgotten, in short looking at each other face to face, confronting each other, laughing around a table at a bar without social media distractions. I could not help but notice the substantial differences between yesterday and today. Before we looked into each other's eyes, we confronted each other, we discussed, we spoke with the people who were part of our world, however today, despite the help of technology, the latter has decreased the time to devote to friends and family. Based on that contradictory thought, at that moment I felt happy to relive those precious years.

That night I couldn't fall asleep easily. I thought about everything that had happened in such a short time. I had met the immense Freddie Mercury, and in front of him, with my spontaneity, I had felt so small and naive. We hadn't even realize that we had attended Freddie's most extraordinary birthday so far, when the next day someone sent us another invitation to a special party in his honor in the German city of Ulm, in the famous nightclub Aquarium on Kohlgasse, in half an hour from Munich. I doubted that someone had a hand in this second invitation. Of course my friends never turned down invitations to parties, especially when it came to their favorite singer.

I knew that Freddie also had a special relationship with Ulma, as Ralf Grimminger writes in his book Nice Society, and was close friends with Garry and Manfred, the owners of the club.

The venue staff were elegantly dressed. Furnished with tables covered with white tablecloths and transparent or wooden chairs with a plant next to each one, it gave the impression of a quiet place where, unlike the other evening, I immediately felt at ease.

Freddie showed up in a tuxedo. I don't know how he managed to travel on the train in that uncomfortable clothing, so when he went on stage he took it off, remaining in white jeans and bare-chested for the pleasure of those present.

I didn't know if it was my sensation or if it was true, but I felt observed in every little movement. The evening was definitely quiter than that of September 5th. People sipped drinks in small groups, one of which I joined. They argued heatedly about mutual friends, one of whom had betrayed another by revealing a secret of his. Suddenly I heard Paul approaching, almost without being noticed, and he murmured exactly these words in my ear: "And what are you hiding?"

"Nothing" I replied, turning my head and finding myself *vis a vis* with him. I looked him straight in the eye.

"Jim asked me to take your backpack to the Studios. Falling out of the back seat it burst open and everything in it spilled over, and a device (he meant cell phone) turned on due to the impact. I saw an image of Queen. I'm sure you can give me a valid explanation", he said in an almost menacing voice.

"That's a kind of kaleidoscope, yeah...that's right, um...the image you noticed is simply a drawing that, when the apparatus is shaken, multiplies into smaller images" I invented then and there, referring to the photo taken with the four children who played each member of Queen, during the filming of *The Miracle*.

"I wonder why I don't believe you" he was direct, without taking his frog-like gaze away, as if to scare me.

"It's really him speaking who, with his declarations to the Sun in 1987 made the figure of an infamous man", I thought, but obviously I couldn't tell him anything, because even he didn't yet know what he was going to do. But we were in 1985 and perhaps he thought that his being so despicable would not come out over the years.

"Anyway, you're always in time to do it, because I haven't said anything to Freddie yet."

"Even I haven't revealed the truth about the glass you secretly gave him two nights ago", I replied firmly, letting him know that I wasn't afraid of the challenge he was throwing at me. "If you believe you are the King who can destroy the Queen, you are very wrong, because she moves freely, unlike you, and you know that the moment you try and do it, you are going to too. The White Queen is protected by the bishops and their horses," I added, aware that all this was truly becoming a kind of dangerous game, in which one wrong move could cost you dearly.

He slipped away amazed at what he had just heard and with a captivating smile that left me baffled. Sonia, Luca and Frank immediately understood my upset and proposed to smoke a cigarette, trying to distract me, telling about a boy who had gotten drunk and laughing heartily. Having learned about it through other people, they told me that Freddie had shot the video for the single *Living on My Own* to Herndrson's. They wanted to distract me, but I was very upset by Paul's intrusiveness. Occasionally I lit a cigarette, but I refused to smoke. As we moved near a plam tree, I saw the latter talking intimately with Freddie and I still felt as if they were looking at me. I was curious to know if he had told him everything or if he wanted to continue his game alone, to then be the usual "good friend".

Above us were four-leaf clovers and a row of hung flags of different states. I looked for the one from my country, Albania, red with a black two-headed eagle, and also that from Italy, because I feel half italian too, but I couldn't find them. Behind my back I heard Freddie's soft voice.

"Oh dear! We don't always find everything we're looking for" and he offered me a *silk out*.

"Thanks Freddie, but I don't smoke."

"You don't smoke, you don't drink…but where do you come from, may I know? From another planet?" he joked.

"Definitely not like Mercury", I said as my friends laughed at the impromptu joke.

"I like you, you have a sense of humour", Freddie replied as he sipped a Heineken.

"No, come on, I was joking, I'm exactly from the distant 2021" I said in a low voice, close to his ear, so that only he would listen, as if that year represented a place. It wasn't clear from my voice if I was still making jokes or if I was serious. However, I probably didn't want to run away from the truth and confrontation. My conscience forced me to be sincere, while the fear of judgment and the fact that I couldn't be understood kept me in check.

"And what about 2021? He asked with the look of someone who didn't know whether to believe me or not.

"We travel through the net" was my answer, again said in a way that I couldn't tell if it was a joke or the truth.

Tell the truth, the first internet domain was registered on March 15, 1985, but it was not immediately available to everyone, so I thought that the term was not yet in common use.

"Very cool the girl" he raised his voice so that the others could hear him too. No one have been following our conversation, so they did not understand what he was taking about.

"Rudi, my name is Rudi" I reinforced.

"Ah, I know, I know, I remember. But it's a boy's name…it doesn't suit you".

"I like it."

And to continue his discourse on my femininity, he added: "You look like a *Nymph in yellow*" looking at my yellow dress with thin blue stripes that showed the colors of my basketball team.

"What a quaere fellow", I continued the lines of *The Fairy Feller's Master-Stroke*. "It's one of my favorite songs. However, in Albanian it is said nimfa."

"Oh yes! I like nimfa. It's beautiful nimfa" he repeated trying to pronounce this word differently from English, while someone from behind called and turned to speak to him.

After a few minutes I saw the hostesses arrive from a distance.

"Hey Fred" I called his firtst name confidentially, even though I knew he didn't like that nickname. We approached when one of the waiters was putting a beautiful cake on the table.

"That's why you called me Fred" he said looking at the guitar-shaped cake. "Brian calls me like this and even if I don't like it, he keeps doing it, one day I'll make that bastard pay" and he laughed while the others, pointing to the names of the parts of the instrument, chose which piece of cake they wanted.

"I'd like the keyboard" someone said and the other followed.

"I'd like the nut" added Sonia.

"Who wants the shoulder?"

"Me" replied Luca laughing.

"The bridge, *please!*"

"I want the strings…"

"You eat so little, are you on diet?"

"And what piece do you want?" he said turning to me.

"The hole" I replied ironically and everyone laughed.

"Then she's the one who doesn't smoke, drink or eat. Oh! Don't be ridiculous" and she laughed out loud. As a result, everyone laughed. A very confidential atmosphere was created.

We looked at each other like two old friends and continued to laugh in complicity, and this time Freddie didn't put his hand over his mouth. We had recently discovered a point in common that was really bringing us closer: irony and self-irony, and in order not to lose the trust that was being created, I wanted to be honest with him.

The blowing on the candles seemed like a light wind that swept away the dust making thoughts clear, generating the right actions. In the smell they left, the reaction of the oxygen in the air, combined with the carbon in the wax, remained. The truth or the lie? That was the question that had been floating around in my head since I was there.

The gifts were all to his liking, on the other hand everyone knew his refined tastes. I hadn't been able to give him mine two days earlier due to how events had gone, so I took advantage of the second invitation:

"Come on, Mr Feller, crack it open if you please" I quoted a line from the song inspired by a painting by Richard Dadd. I could tell from his look and smile that he was surprised at how I used the lyrics of his songs at the right times.

He unwrapped the gift with the joy of a child, with the impatience of a teenager and the anticipation of an adult. He raised it slightly for those around him to see. From the look I perceived the strangeness of receiving a wristwatch as a gift, or rather a smartwatch with sapphire crystal, but no one knew the name of that object or even how it worked. He looked at it in amazement: that was a present for my fiftieth birthday that I had never used. It is no coincidence that I thought of giving it to him to achieve my goal.

It wouldn't have been to his liking, knowing he didn't wear them and moreover knowing his refined tastes in vintage items, but that modern object never seen before aroused his curiosity.

"Stachel, this does not work, darling" he said after the German bad word, thinking it was a joke. He put it to his ear to hear the tick tock, looked at it sideways to see if there were buttons to get it going, but then gave up and impatiently left it on the table.

"It works. I'll show you how to operate it later" I said apparently reassuring, but it was just a ploy to save me from the situation.

I would turn it on when the times was right. Having given him a watch that was not currently active was like wanting to stop time to always see him happy, carefree and above all in good health.

While he calmly continued to unwrap the other presents, I stepped aside and went to look for my fellow adventurers, who were watching the scene not far from us. As I joined them, I caught Paul's suspicious gaze as he shook his head. I changed it back with an ironic laugh followed by a grimace.

The evening went on quietly, and around three in the morning we decided to leave. We went to say hello to everyone and finally Freddie too, who told me I was welcome Musicland if I wanted to come back. I thanked him heartily, squeezing his hand tightly. He gave off a light like his whole being "incandescent", in contrast with the blue of the Danube that flowed majestically outside.

I woke up late that Sunday. I thought that I would have loved to become friend with Freddie, but for as I perceive it, the bond of friendship is meant to be honest and clean, and to get to that I should have confess everything I knew.

***

I spent the month of September among studies and numerous activities, carried out in the time left free from daily lessons and on weekends, trips, visits to museums and monuments. Among the works that stuck in my memory were the old *(Altes)* and the new *(Neues)* Town Hall of Munich, the Royal Palace, the Cathedral of Our Lady *(Dom zu Unserer Lieben Frau)*, and the English Garden of Munich. All this allowed me to master the language and to socialize with students from other countries as well as Sonia and Luca, (an engaged couple of Italian origins) and Frank of British nationality, with whom I shared the house. I also met other guys, like Katy, Annarita, Joseph and Gabriel. Together we shared a passion for Queen's music. As the days went by, my mind seemed like a hive in which the buzz of thoughts sought a selection of the chronology of events to report to Freddie, even if the truthful triumphed among the contradictory ones. I was aware that I had to do the right thing and the time ahead of me had to turn only in my favor. I was so convinced that at the end of October I decided to visit him again at the Studios.

Mack Reinhold, one of the record producers of several albums and a close friend of Freddie, opened the door for me and told me to wait. I knew he stood as godfather to his youngest son, nemed Little Freddie. I sat down when I realized that behind me there was a large glass framed in light brown wood, that divided the liveroom from the room where I was.

I got so close that the glass fogged up because I couldn't believe my eyes. The four Queen were there. I didn't understand whether they could see me on the other side or not, but that didn't stop me from clinging to the glass. Where could such an occasion happen to me again? I observed them in minute detail. Roger's drumsticks had his name on them, as did Brian's guitar.

"One flash of light yeah, one god, one vision"
Freddie was singing *One Vision* with an indescribable passion, a four-person choir that seemed like a complex of many people put together, laughing like never before.

Freddie was wearing jeans and a tank top with narrow black and white stripes. He tossed the headphones in the air and caught them on the fly. He then made the gesture of playing the drums and Roger winked.
"They're really fun" I thought and smiled like a little girl. I backed away because John jokingly seemed to be looking my way and Brian was doing the same too. I didn't understand if on the other side there was a glass-mirror, or simply a glass from which they too could see who was in the monitor room. I didn't want them to see me, so I could watch the recordings until the end. Freddie went wild in

front of the drums with Roger pounding hard. After a while the latter stuck out his tongue, took off his glasses and started scratching his head, while his place on drums was taken by John. They all made funny faces and I started laughing too, as Mack laughed heartily as he lowered his head over the mixer. It was impossible to resist Queen.

With my finger I wrote the number 1 on the fogged glass with an arrow above it. A few moments later, I saw Freddie emerge from a side door: he was excited and greeted me enthusiastically, pointing a finger at my track on the glass. They were number one.

"Hello darling!"

"Hi Fredie!" no matter how hard I tried, my doubles always left something to be desired, precisely because there are no double consonants in my language. *"How are you?"*

He replied that he was fine and that he was delighted with the new single, *One Vision*, which would be released in November.

"Now let's take a short break, come dear, I'll offer you something at the bar inside here."

It was the last days of autumn and Munich was already feeling the cold, so we decided to have his favorite tea, *Earl Grey* with a little milk and two sugar cubes, just the way he liked it, and like two good friends we sat down to have a chat. Freddie was very respectful. He asked me how my studies were going and between one talk and another we also remembered things from our childhood. I told him that I, like him, had been collecting stamps since I was 8 years old.

"I also have a Royal Mail stamp, from the *Millennium Stamp* series, showing you at Live in Australia in Sydney, in April of this year", I said, leaving him a little perplexed.

"Royal Mail? I don't know anything about this stamp. Then I'll find out better. Are you sure?"

"Mmm… maybe I'm getting confused" I replied.

When I had Freddie in front of me I didn't understand anything anymore. I slipped into another revelation. Obviously the stamp had come out in 1999, but luckily this time too I was quick to change the subject immediately, asking him if he wanted to play a game of ping-pong, pointing to a card table in the back corridor. I would spend hours and hours playing ping-pong in my school's lecture hall with my high school friend Miranda. She was a champion and it was she who taught me. Freddie could play very well too since his school days.

"I bet I win" I said inviting him to play.

In no time we found ourselves facing each other with rackets in hand. Maybe he needed to take a break. Freddie laughed at the way I held it, between thumb and forefinger without making a fist.

"It's called a pen style and it's used by the Chinese and the Japanese" I explained. "There…you go…even often…to Japan…you should…know." I was talking in spurts as I hopped and hit the ball. Instead he tried to imitate me and laughed because he couldn't shoot like this.

"Look, I'm ahead" I tried to increase the competition.

At that moment there was harmony between us and I didn't want to interrupt the pleasure of being in his company, but that day I returned with other intentions.

"If I can decide to tell everything, I want it to be today" I thought when, just like in soap operas, someone interrupts at the climax, Macke approached and politely asked if he was ready to continue. Freddie nodded, then turned to me:

"My dear, you are very good. We will continue another time, I promise you": then he added: "We have to finish recording *One Vision*."

"I know dear. *I have a dream*" I pronounced the title of one of Martin Luther King's most famous speeches, which inspired the band for the lyrics of that song. Among other things, the passage began with a phrase pronounced bakwards, namely "*God works in mysterious ways... mysterious ways*", words that recalled those of the author himself.

Not knowing when I would see Freddie again, I knowingly told him this time in order to arouse a little more curiosity in him, which for a moment was baffled. I couldn't tell what he was thinking at that precise moment, if asking me "How do you know?" or "What dream do you have?". I just know that he looked me straight in the eyes and didn't say a word. Instead my gaze said it all. paradoxically I was happy and sad at the same time. I hugged him suddenly without him expecting it. After a few seconds I felt the warmth of his arms and his scent.

"See you soon".

Freddie walked off at a fast pace, followed by his producer. I didn't want to leave, so I stayed for a few more minutes at the previous station, to watch the continuation of the recordings. Freddie proposed to do the second part. As a good perfectionist, he tried to make others understand that the right adjective was needed before the word decision. They were trying to agree.

I turned to Macke who with his gaze seemed to ask me: "Still here?"

I replied anyway: "Another minute and I leave" and he approved with a nod.

Freddie resumed singing. Something didn't add up while Roger said otherwise. Then he had Roger try, who cut off a whole piece. They laughed. Brian was making funny faces. They continued to record.

"One man, one goal, one true religion,
One shit, one asshole, two boobs.. John Deacon"

They laughed a lot that day, and inevitably those around them did too. I too got infected.

I had done well not to interrupt this harmony that existed among the boys. Maybe it wasn't the right time yet or maybe I wasn't ready, otherwise I would have insisted. Give time to time, they say. I decided to walk back.

The incessant rain could not shake off my sense of duty. The drops that descended from my wavy black hair gave it a particular reflection. They were similar to those of Freddie in the video clip of *Play the Game*, in 1980, where he laughs as they throw water on him. I was so excited that I realized I was all wet only when I felt the first shivers of cold. As I quickened my pace, I sensed someone approaching. I looked at him out of the corner of my eye. Every now and then he lowered his big black umbrella so as not to be recognized. Surely it was one of Paul's men, but he proved me wrong when he turned into a narrow street just before I arrived at my flat; but the doubt hadn't vanished, because at first it seemed like a strategy and this stalking didn't scare me, because it was what I felt like doing: telling Freddie everything that had happened after that cursed 1991, even at my risk. Then I firmly believe that we would all like to know what will happen when we are gone: what others will say, if they will remember us, or how they will do it…

And while these questions occupied my thoughts, I found myself near the street where I lived. As soon as I entered the house I took a hot shower and started studying. Sonia, Luca and Frank had gone away for a slightly longer weekend. The days flowed quite calmly among the various commitments, until one Saturday after going to meet other friends, on my return I found the door wide open and the house ransacked. I was immediately reminded of the man who had followed me back from Musicland Studios. I immediately went to the rummage in the mess of things thrown on the floor and immediately realized that Jim's book was missing. I confirmed my doubt that it was one of Paul's men when I heard the message left on the answering machine.

"Hello, I'm Paul. I should speak to you, miss. Meet you tomorrow at 5 pm at the Hofgarten, inside the Temple of Diana."

I was silent for a long time thinking about what to do. I had little time left to design a strategy. I immediately called my three friends, who were available as always and anticipated their return. I had to explain to them my journey into the past and what my mission was. Even if they remained petrified, they supported me right away.

"Here I am, my friend" Sonia's voice warmed me.

As always, we understood each other immediately with a glance. Our telepathy was something extraordinary.

"We must recover the book at all costs" I said. "It's very important".

That book, called *My years with Freddie Mercury*, was published a few years ago, but I bought it in 2019. This was the most compelling evidence in Pauls' hands. I had to stop him from showing it to Freddie. I prayed God he hadn't done it yet. I preferred to do it in person at the right time.

Studying the map of the meeting place in detail, we defined an action plan that was to prove successful in achieving the goal. All that remained was to wait.

At about 4 pm we took the subway, which stopped near the garden, in the center of Munich, which was truly a place of peace. The flowerbeds full of colorful flowers, the fountains and people af all ages playing bowls, gave a touch of joy to this place even if the sky was cloudy.

We went aroung in circles to better study the return routes. As the day grew shorter, the walks and benches emptied. We approached the Temple of Diana where the tango musicians and dancers were packing their bags to leave. I looked around anxiously and my gaze met Sonia's, who clenched her fist to give me courage.

"If you know the enemy and yourself, your victory is sure" this sentence of the wise Sun Tzu came to my mind and I forced myself to face the situation that had arisen.

Paul showed up at the temple like clockwork. As expected, he was not alone, with him there were two men dressed as bodyguards, one of whom stopped slightly behind, surely to have a wider field of vision, even though each of the eight arches led to the garden. Paul didn't even wait for the last violinist to leave. He started counting all the objects and words that made him doubt me. He told me that if I didn't tell him the truth, he would tell Freddie everything.

"Thank goodness, he hasn't done it yet", I thought with relief.

"If you tell me what you know, you'll get a nice reward" he tried to bribe me.

"Would you like to pay me with the money you earned thanks to Freddie?" I joked. I proudly replied that this matter did not concern him, that he had to stop following me and that I did not need his money. "If there's something to reveal, I'll do it personally with Freddie" I added decisively and looked at him contemptuously.

He pulled the book out of his pocket with one hand and gave me the *loser* sign with the other. He understood that he was out of the game and he didn't like it. If he hadn't given it to him yet, there was a reason. It was time to act. Frank, hidden behind one of the temple, turned the stereo connected to the speakers at full volume and Freddie's powerful voice in *Flick of the Whrist* made Paul tremble.

Don't look back!
It's a rip-off
Flick of the wrist and you're dead, baby

Paul, petrified, turned his head in the direction of the voice, despite the order of Freddie, who seemed to be behind him.

"When the opponent has many loose pieces, the Queen makes double attacks", I reminded him of the rules of the game.

The neighing of the horses made him tremble with fear. Joseph and Katy, horse enthusiasts, had lent us their horses, to be able to escape as quickly as possible.

"Check mate!" I shouted, while on the opposite side Luca also got into action and, with a Karate move, threw down the book which Sonia caught on the fly.

He could not destroy the Queen because she was protected by horses. At that moment we felt like the proudest bishops on earth. Only the union between the two would have saved her.

They kept running towards us, more and more fierce. We passed through the garden which connected Odeonsplatz with the Englischer Garden. The latter was an expanse of meadows and trees. As soon as we entered we found ourselves at Kleinhessoloer See, an artificial lake fed by the Eisbach river, where our two accomplices were waiting for us, and to whom we returned the horses. Katy, being a big fan of Freddie, recommended that I send him a greeting from her. "Even a kiss", she added.

"It twill be done. And thanks for the help, guys."

As they set off, we, as planned, took one of those pedal boats that they rented during the day to go around the lake. Everything that was happening was as surreal as it was funny. We laughed at the way we'd managed to reclaim the book. And while Paul's men became two black dots in the distance, we sang out loud *"You don't fool me"* laughing with joy.

It was a devilishly funny plan, created by four guys with no bad intentions.

As soon as we got off we walked on the paths of the English park, and along the way we found the Chinesischer Turm, the Chinese tower 25 meters high, and later, on the hill, we could see Monopteros, a fake Greek temple, and we climbed to the top to admire the panorama of the whole park. It looked like the siege tower from where we felt safe. If the chess game started with four rooks, ours ended with one. With the lightness of our years we felt like winners.

A few days later I heard the single *One Vision*, which entered the charts on November 12 of that year, and I was pleased to think that I had witnessed part of the recording. I would have liked to congratulate Freddie personally, but four days earlier he had flown to London to record a demo of *The Great Pretender*, at composer Mike Moran's London residence.

Part of the study holiday was coming to an end together with the current year. As I listened to *Thank God It's Christmas*, the Christmas song that topped the charts for six weeks over the festive period in early 1985, then briefly returned to the charts again in the UK in 1995 with a new video clip, I thought: "Where will I spend the holidays?". If I stayed in Munich I would have had to celebrate the upcoming new year, 1986, and if I had returned home I would have made the leap into the future by celebrating 2022. Even though I leaned more towards the first option, I still missed my real life. Involuntarily the person who decided where I was going to spend New Year's Eve was Sonia, who called to tell me that Frank had invited us to his house in London for the holidays. I absolutely could not refuse. It was a good opportunity to be in the company of friends and visit the capital of England. The last days in Munich went by so quickly that I found myself with my suitcase in hand to greet and thank this beautiful German city for the study program it had offered me and, moreover, for letting me meet Freddie.

***

London, December 1985

    I was mesmerized by the Christmas lights of London. The more bizarre ones shone in the 13 streets of the beautiful Carnaby area. We took a panoramic bus for a night tour of the city and see them up close. We continued the "tour of lights" with a bag of roasted chestnuts in hand along the Thames, and then we enjoyed a cruise along with Santa Claus. We were fascinated by the beauty of the Christmas trees and the atmosphere of Hyde Park. Finally we went skating under the Winterville ferris wheel in Clapham Common.

    The next day was dedicated to gifts, shows, Christmas classics at the Cinema in the Snow and outdoor theaters. I was thinking that in a few months I would have to return to my future life, when a green caterpillar with a red head caught my attention. Silently, I stopped in front of the puppe theater that animated children's writer Eric Carle's *The Very Hungry Caterpillar*. I thought of my nursery children, of my sacrifices among studies and sports to get to do the job I liked best of all. It was pleasant and too good to relive my youth again, but the future was "the place" where I wanted to continue my life. I had a moment of nostalgia and the desire to embrace my loved ones again.

    I really needed to sit down and sip mulled wine. We were tired of traveling all over London. In the morning we had gone shopping at Harrods department store, where we had not missed the opportunity to taste the delicious Christmas *pudding* and *mince pie* from its famous food stalls. Agreeing on the desire to spend the evening in a pub, we opted for the Xenon, and arriving at 195 Piccadilly, we found ourselves in a very busy place. A central light shot out rays of sun, and the other colored ones were precisely in Christmas theme. This was the place frequented not only by Queen, but also by other artists such as George

Michael, Madonna, Samantha Fox, Whitney Houston, Prince and many others.

"Last year Freddie celebrated his 38th birthday here", said Sonia, who was always in the know about where Freddie and Queen frequented in London.

"Oh yes, I had read about it in a magazine, the cake in the shape of a red Roll Royce. The way Freddie held the knife was very funny, it looked like he was going to stab it" added Frank, and we laughed imagining the scene.

"The rest of Queen and all the friends he lived with at Garden Lodge, were there too. Everyone was wearing jackets, only Freddie was in a tank top. He was never cold," I commented, after finding a magazine nearby with photos of that event. "How nice to be in a place frequented by Queen" I added, as I looked around, eager to see Freddie again. "Lately it seems that we are chasing each other. I wonder if any of them will be there tonight" I made a wish that unfortunately didn't come true.

I thought about sending Freddie a postcard, but the idea of Paul knowing I was in London, didn't excite me. I needed quiet for the moment. At this time of the year it was as if I had abandoned the idea of completing my mission as a secret revealer. We had a wonderful Crhristmas, and we got on so well that Frank suggested we stay a few more months, since his parents had another house at our disposal. This way we would have had the opportunity to perfect our English and to see London calmly. The time that passed while we were discovering this beautiful city was not perceived, and so I found myself at the beginning of June at the Cartier shop, to buy a present for Sonia's birthday, when I heard a familiar voice with an unmistakable pronunciation, a bit like mine with Italian. We were both from behind but with the corner of my eye I recognized him immediately. "Oh God, Freddie." I continued to look at what was displayed in the bright windows with the hope that he would not recognize me, when I felt a hand on my shoulder.

I turned around in slow motion and exclaimed in feigned surprise: "Freddie!" trying to hide the embarassment.

"*Hello darling!* What are you doing here?" he said, showing amazement at seeing me. "Have you come to buy another watch?" He had one of his laughs and continued: "Those watches you give away, you can't find them here... *anyaway*."

"I came here by accident. I've never been to this shop before. I'm supposed to get my friend a present for her birthday on June 11, but I guess I'll just buy something else. I'll go to Harrods or Biba, there's more choice and it's cheaper. I've seen enough for today. It's too hot to walk around."

"Darling, may I know how long have you been in London?" he asked .

"A few weeks ago", I lied.

"Oh baby! But you could have come to see me. We're friends now, aren't we?"

"Dear! I honestly didn't know where you live" I told him.

"You'll know from now on though, because I bought a house in Kensington. Indeed, I invite you to the party that I will give in September, even if it is reserved for a few, feel free to bring your friends, so you will teach me how to turn on the clock you gave me."

"We will be there for sure...and right now what are you doing as a band?"

"Oh dear, on June 6th the *Magic Tour* starts from Stockholm, and just on your friend's birthday we are in Leiden, in the Netherlands. The last concert will be at Knebworth Park."

"I saw that there is no stage in Italy", I said with great regret. "Freddie, there are thousands of fans who go crazy for Queen."

"Oh dear, we will also come to Italy on another occasion, even if I don't have a good memory of Sanremo festival. Shit, they forcet us to playback."

"Everyone understood it when you purposely raised the microphone, but continued to sing. You're too cool, darling."

He wasn't entirely wrong. Anyway, I thought it would be nice to see one of these stages, when my thought was interrupted:

"Now, while I'm shopping, my chauffeur Tarry could take you home, since you've finished your rounds for today."

"Thanks Freddie! You are always so kind and thoughtful to me."

We said goodbye. He looked at me with a sense of protection, like an older brother. By now I thought his doubts had vanished. Getting into his favorite car, the Rolls Royce registered WLX 293M, gave me unique sensations.

Six months had passed and perhaps Paul too had forgotten everything about me and my secrets. However, I could not decline the invitation to the Garden Lodge party. I liked the theme parties that Freddie organized and I wanted to be there at all costs.

On Sonia's birthday, a courier knocked on the door and delivered me a parcel. We eagerly opened it together and found two separate packets and a greeting card for her and another one for me.

"That's why he had his chauffeur drive me", I thought of his attempt to find out where I lived. Freddie was really umpredictable. He gave Sonia a bracelet with a queen's crown hanging on it, and for me there was a watch accompanied by a piece of paper in which it was written:

"You can't invest the watch, you can't make time to go back, it's not a penalty". Without thinking about the message he wanted to send us with these words, we jumped like springs and started to screaming with joy.

There were also four front row tickets for the August 9 concert at Knebworth Park, north London, the last leg of the *Magic Tour*. At the end of May I had seen the advertisement in the newspaper, but it was immediately sold out and I no longer hoped to participate in this concert. When Freddie involved, however, the surprises never ended.

A few months later I would have turned 18, while Freddie was about 40. Ours was a friendship that was growing slowly and the thought of breaking down the barriers among past, present and future began to grow in me. I had just had the last opportunity to put my conscience at ease and to understand if Freddie would be happy with everything that was going to happen in the rest of his life. I felt the duty to represent all the fans, and to find the most appropriate way to tell them everything I knew; what had happened afterwards: events, feelings, dedications, memories...if I had told him now, could I have changed the course of his life? Maybe Freddie would have made other choices? But what was I thinking? Destiny can't be changed for anyone, but how I wish it could.

I don't remember a summer flying by as quickly as that of '86, even though it was still early August. Early in the morning on 9th August we took the train from King's Cross Station. We were thrilled. In half an hour we arrived at Knebworth Park, an English village in northern Hertfordshire, just south of Stevenage, where people flocked. Many mounted police officers and others in cars were in charge of security. From the density of the traffic, the magnitude of the event was perceived. A bridge similar to the shape of a delta, but a little rounder, packed with cars, led to a single road that led to the huge park. Unfortunately, being the only road, a congestion that inevitably blocked the normal road traffic formed, so we took the opportunity to stop at the *Fish & Chips bar* for a quick breakfast.

At about nine o'clock the audience began to enter the park. I held tightly those notes, on which was written: *"9th August, 1986 New Musical Express, Queen, Status Quo, Big Country, Knebworth Park",* which even after years would remain living proof of that day. Above our heads the G-DHTL helicopter carrying Queen, after having crossed the Thames and the legendary Battersea Power Station, painted in the same way as the cover of the album *A Kind of Magic,* was flying over a gigantic sea of people. As far as I knew, there were about two hundred thousand of us.

I wished I was a fly inside the helicopter, to observe the reaction of Queen in seeing such a huge crowd of people before their eyes. I directed my gaze to the sky, from where our idols would soon descend. There were many, thousands, in waiting certainly not Belouis Some, who opened the concert in the afternoon, and not even Big Country and Status Quo who continued, but the most popular band of the moment, Queen, who amid boos, screams and fan cheers began with *One Vision.*

The audience was in frenzy. There were shouts, laughter and whistles. Freddie came in, wearing his yellow jacket, holding the microphone with both hands and addressed the crowd: *"Is everybody ok? Having a nice day? Yeah, not too bad... hey, now you gonna put up with us"*

The concert continued with *In the Laps of the Gods,* and later *Seaven Seas of Rhye.* Freddie wiped the sweat with a white towel and took off his jacket, leaving himself with a tank top of the same color, and started singing *A Kind of Magic.* After that he interacted with those present through his *"Eeeeoooo".* He came closest to us singing

Under Pressure, followed by *Another One Bites the Dust.* We were in the middle of summer, it was very hot and he was constantly drying himself. He also did so during a slightly longer speech:

"You know for three months that this is the last leg of our tour, do you know it or not? It's such a beautiful way to end it, I mean, look! Many of you might even add that this was the best European tour yet. Thanks to all of you, and all the assholes out there. Earlier there were rumors about us breaking up soon, fuck it, fuck it! Look at this, how could we separate if we have such an audience? We're not that stupid."

It was dark now. At the first notes of *I Want to Break Free,* I expected to see him wearing a black skirt and pink sleeveless shirt, but it wasn't like that. Invited by Freddie, fans sang along with him. Finally he raised the microphone with both hands above his head. He returned with one of his vocalizations, where the total mastery of the voice is perceived even by those who know nothing of music. Great. He left the stage for a small break, which was filled with a long solo from Brian. Then he came back with *Now I'm Here.* Yes, we were there and it was great to sing *Love of My Life* with him. Just a classical guitar and his unmistakable voice. He motioned for the fans to sing along, then stopped, letting the fans continue. *"Fabulous!"* he exclaimed and continued: *"Do you remember?"*

I will surely always remember this night.

Jokingly he said these words: *"I still fuckin' love you".* Then he finished: *"Love of my life, uuu jee eeeee".* A fan was heard shouting*: "Yeah! Freddie boys".* Roger's voice entered the scene and together with Freddie sang *You're So Square, Mary Lou and Tutti Frutti.*

We were almost at the end and the majestic *Bohemian Rhapsody* could not be missing. We all sang in chorus with our hands raised. Almost in the front row, a girl was wearing a T.shirt with *Queen* on her heart, right where they were for us. At the final song Freddie lowered his head, saluted like a commander at his victory, and bowed to the audience. I thought it was the last song, but with a guitar in hand Freddie continued with *Crazy Little Thing Called Love,* which ended in total darkness for a few minutes and then started again with *Radio Ga Ga.* He said goodbye as he left the stage, then returned with a white cape that looked like a long veil and went wild with *We Will Rock You*. He stripped to his shirt to sing *Friends Will Be Friends and We Are the Champions*.

"*Freddie, you are the champion!*"

We knew the concert was almost over when we saw him in the red cape and king's crown. Under the notes of the English anthem *God Save the Queen*, Freddie thanked his admirers: "*You have been and extraordinary, very special audience. Thank you very much, good night, sweet dreams, we love you.*"

With his right hand he raised the crown and bowed, while the other three Queen with their hands raised greeted their fans, so enthusiastic that they didn't want to move from there.

There are no recordings of this great concert, except something amateurish, but the real recordings are those that remain in the memory of everyone who was present that evening. Sadly it was Queen's last performance with Freddie, but of course they couldn't know that. Once off stage, where Mary was waiting for him, their eyes met. Perhaps they both sensed that Freddie had just finished his last live concert. The lights in the park were turned off, making it very difficult for spectators to get back to their cars. We took the opportunity to go backstage where someone was waiting to wrap them in their bathrobes, almost chasing them. We raised our hands to show ourselves, but they quickly walked away, certainly very sorry for the unfortunate event of that evening, namely the death of a fan. When Freddie found out, he said that if people had to die to go to see them, they wouldn't play any more concerts. I hoped that these words stir the conscience of someone who had committed an unforgivable act, and that it would never be repeated again, in any concert.

Although it was not possible to say goodbye to the band, *A Night of Summer Magic* remained so for us Queen fans.

***

August passed quickly and Sunday, September 7, 1986, the day of the opening party of Garden Lodge, as Freddie nicknamed his enormous mansion, arrived. It was located near a group of artists' houses started by Lord Leighton at Leighton House.

Together with my friends, we went a little earlier than the scheduled time. We did not know the man who opened it for us. We stayed for about ten minutes in the garden. To our left the much discussed cherry tree. At the corner was a magnolia tree, a little further down a kind of greenhouse and a natural pool in which Freddie would put his koi carp in the days to come. I imagined them there as in the photos I had recently seen, when we were invited to enter. Peter Freestone and Jim Hutton asked the boys for help moving a piece of furniture. Freddie called Sonia and I to join Mary and David Wigg on the balcony, for the prank he had set up to spy on the entrance, so he could hear what his friends were saying about the house as they entered.

"For anyone who says something bad, there will never be another invitation" he laughed.

It was too funny being in that situation. I was worse than Freddie when it came to pranking friends. Sitting on our knees we hid on the balcony from which no one could see us. Every time we heard footsteps we wanted to laugh, but we held back so as not to be discovered. At one point,

I took off my bulby hat and stood on tiptoe to see what was happening below. There were many guests, including the members of Queen with their respective women. Then Jim Beach, Reinhold Mack, Tim Rice, Peter Straker and many others also arrived, strictly each with a funny hat on the head. Jim Hutton, who was already in the gardener's shoes, fenced off the pool with candles so that no one would get hurt by falling onto it. While sitting on tiptoe to see who was coming I lost my balance and fell to the floor. The others laughed.

"Ssst... be quiet, otherwise they'll find us."

"Mary! Your fan hat can be seen from below."

"Maybe because I'm tall, it's best if I lie down."

"Then mine would show more" I said considering that we were exactly the same height.

"Ssst! Shut up, they hear us."

We stayed like this until our legs tingled and we decided to join the others. The mission was not accomplished because no one fault the house chosen by Freddie. After all, who could question his indisputable taste?

I pretended to leave, but returned as soon as the others came down. I waited until the end to see if Prenter would come. He didn't and I was relieved.

The party had already begun with the notes of *Jump to It* by Aretha Franklin, one of Freddie's favorite singers, playing in the background. As we went downstairs I saw in one of the rooms the ostrich feather blanket that Freddie used in the video that inspired us to put on our hats. At that moment not even he would have ever imagined that one day he would have used it in such a delicate moment of his life.

Freddie came up and complimented us on our chosen hats. "My dears, these hats are outstanding. Whose idea was it?" he asked, pointing his finger at the bananas on Luca's head and giggling.

"Im going slightly mad" Luca replied.

"He's not serious, that is, he's not going crazy" I immediately intervened. "Come on Luca, don't overdo it!"

"No, I was referring to the video in which a blond boy had a hat in the shape of a teapot, the same as Frank's, and another one as a joker" continued Luca who, not being a fan of Queen at the moment, did not remember the names of Roger and John. He also didn't know that the video I showed him on videotape had only been released in '91.

As soon as he uttered the word "joker", Freddie whirled around to face me and as I lifted my multicolored tricorn hat, which had gone down due to the weight, his gaze met mine, quite ridiculous and embarassing.

"Dear! Can you tell me more?"

"There was a misunderstanding...because...I told the guys that it would be cool if you and the other Queen wore our hats in an upcoming video clip to look a little crazy, different than usual" I said as I squeezed my fingers cross.

"You know darling, that wouldn't be a bad idea" he said just to please me and walked away towards Peter Straker, to whom, as I later learned, he had asked to simulate with Roger the backing vocal parts in the video of *The Great Pretender*, which resumed a year later, in 1987.

I was in a cold sweat, but also this time Freddie didn't seem to give much importance to the words. Obviously he didn't have the idea of that video yet, in which in addition to those hats there would also have been a monkey, a penguin, daffodils, but if he had found out I would have had to give him an explanation.

Even after the party, he spent the night joking with David downstairs, while Phoebe and Jim rested to tackle tomorrow's work, which was putting the koi in the pond.

Kindly, Freddie had offered everyone, in case they were unable to get home, to spend the night at Garden Lodge. We could not refuse. Indeed, it was the right opportunity to find the watch I had given him and put it to work.

While the remaining few went to sleep, I started taking a peek at the house under the guise of going to the bathroom, and I was actually getting inside when, passing the door, I saw Johnson & Johnson baby shampoo, and I remembered reading on Peter Freestone's blog that Freddie used just that, because he had very delicate skin like a baby. His oversized exotically patterned towels and Roger et Gallet soaps in all frangrances, were prominently displayed. I went over to smell those *au chaudron* and *bois d'arange*, which were missing from my collection. Next to the bars of soap were his favorite perfumes, *Monsieur* and *L'Interdit* by Givenchy. As I put on some Clarins *Eau Dynamisante*, I felt an immediate freshness that reminded me of the perfume I had smelled when I hugged him. Silently I walked upstairs, where Freddie's room was. Curious, I peeked out the door. To the left was a bed with a brightly colored white angora base blanket over it with circular designs, and a living area to the right with a modern couch and chaise longue. On the wall hung a pretty portrait of a woman by the pre-Raphaelite artist Tissot. Several paintings by Louis Icart decorated the walls and lots of crystal objects, porcelain, Lalique boxes and Japanese lacquered boxes filled the French windows. After discreetly searching one of them, I found the smartwatch. I turned it on, entered the pin, and placed it on the nightstand next to his bed.

In the suite the walls were covered with gold and platinum records. Near the stairs leading up to his room was a library, and although he didn't like to read, there was no shortage of classic books, dictionaries and encyclopedias. The next door was the entrance to the guest suite, the walls of which were lined with surrealist works by Dali.

Seeing something that took me to many years later, was like remembering where I had come from. This painter reminded me of my favorite series, *La Casa de Papel,* which I used to watch with my youngest daughter, on the days when we couldn't leave the house during the lockdown, we still had to finish watching it. This nostalgia tha suddenly appeared consumed me. I didn't want to think about it...

It was now night and I was wondering if we could stay there. For a year now, I felt like I was living in a dream. Meeting Freddie at first by pure chance, and later for the little friendship we had made, having attended his birthdays and being in his new home, was like living a parallel reality in which every event left an indescribable emotion. Recovering from my thoughts, I continued to explore that relaxing pastel-colored environment.

At the top of the stairs leading to the kitchen was a sound room where Freddie kept a collection of albums and videos, as well as a mahogany and maple bar. Behind the wall of the bar hung a huge picture with a painting of the jungle by the painter Rudi Patterson.

Going down I found myself in front of a large living room with huge windows, a marble fireplace, a sofa, two comfortable armchairs and a large television. How many times will he have seen his favorite films here: S*ome like it Hot, Women* and other comedies...I imagined him in good company as always laughing and joking, but my imagination stopped when I saw that object of enormous artistic value, placed near the window, which had made the history of music.

"Oh my God! *Bohemian Rhapsody's piano!*"

He played Beethoven's *Impromptu* when Montsy came to visit him. From the large windows, the lights from the garden penetrated the semi-dark room, so I went over to have a better look at it. Touching the keyboard, a note started and in the meantime I felt someone tug at my arm.

"I've been looking for you for half an hour" said Sonia.

"Oh my! You scared me. I nearly blew up", I replied.

We laughed softly and the silence increased our laughter, which we could no longer hold back. I told her, still in a low voice, that when I came out of the bathroom I had lost my bearings. "This house is so big that I got lost".

Tom's meow made us tremble. In an attempt to run away, it was about to throw down an expensive Tiffany lamp, with the base in the shape of five lily buds, placed on a chest of drawers, which was saved by a miracle.

"Quick, let's continue!" Sonia ordered.

"Wait!" I answered grabbing her by the shirt. I lingered on a painting by Mirò, with his unmistakable style and primary colors, with which I had created so many "masterpieces" with the children at nursey school. There was always some detail reminding me that my journey was ending and my return to the future was near.

We passed through a set of double doors.

"Stop Sonia! Look! The Japanese room" I exclaimed in atonishment.

Here we took a quick look: kinomos, multicolored paintings, pieces of furniture, prints from the studios of Utamaro artists. An artwork called *A Lover of Children,* hanging sideways, belonged to one of the latter. Numerous lacquered objects and miniature sculptures were housed in a showcase, decorated with oriental motifs. On a small table full of photos, positioned near the wall, there was a painting titled W*oman after the bath,* by Goyo Hashiguchi, a Japanese artist, known for the shin-hanga movement and author of several masterpieces.

The room had a particular aspect that was visually striking, and it was proof of Freddie's passion for Japan.

He had brought a piece of this beautiful country to his home.

We approached the entrance where there were two more doors. One belonged to the kitchen, where the black and white rhombus tiles like those in my bathroom did not go unnoticed, with the only difference that mine were square. I had always had my own idea of shapes, because seen from another angle the squares looked like rhombuses and viceversa. Metaphorically it was like seeing a concept from different points of view, without changing the content.

From here a staircase led to the upper floors, which led through a back door to the wine cellar. I took one in hand. The bottle was similar to that white wine with the same name that I bought in Montreux, the St Saphorin du Laveau, who knows if Freddie drank the same wine; after all, many years had passed.

In the living room, above the fireplace, a painting by Marc Chagall, *The Judgment of Chloe,* made with gouache (a tempera color made opaque by the addition of white obtained from chalk or arabic range) joined the pastel colors of the other prints colored to match the walls and curtains. A mixture of shades, from saffron yellow to green to red, gave a touch of creativity and an exotic look to what used to be the dining room, in the center of which there was a table for ten people.

We heard voices coming from nearby. Freddie was standing and David in an armchair. At low volume, the soundtrack of the film *Cabaret* was playing.

"Oh, our *girls* don't want to go to bed..."

"Usually I sleep very little, I prefer to do something useful during those hours" I replied.

"Don't tell me, dear. I always considered it a waste of time...Do you want something to drink?"

"Vodka and Schweppes for me" Sonia asked kindly.

"Is Stolichnaya okay, honey?"

"Sure, thank you dear."

"Instead, I would like something sweet at this time" I said.

"There are candies and chocolates on that other table" he said, pointing his finger at Quality Street and Godiva, his favorites.

"I'm not sleepy, but I don't feel like watching a long movie. Shall we watch a funny short film?" I proposed.

Freddie suggested we watch *Tom e Jerry,* and we all agreed. I knew he liked this cartoon. I liked it a lot too, so I didn't hesitate to say yes right away. When I was little, I always watched it with my dad. I felt melancholy rising.

From our laughter in watching that cat and mouse chasing each other, that inner child that lives in each of us with all its spontaneity, enthusiasm and vitality emerged. That child that despite the growth, change and transformation we still kept inside. Meanwhile I continued to eat the candies.

"Sweet tooth...tomorrow I'm sending Phoebe to buy some sweets for breakfast at my favorite bakery at Jane Asher's". On hearing Peter's nickname, I asked him curiously:

"You have this habit of putting nicknames on all your friends, but if you had to give us a nickname, what would you call us?"

"*Darling...* You..." he said turning to Sonia, "I'd call you Mumy. But as for you, dear" he turned to me, saying that he had sometimes doubted me and someone had pushed him to do it more, "I think *You don't know*" .

"Like *Lily doesn't know*, the lily of the valley" I immediately grasped the concept, which however did not correspond to reality, because I knew too much. I thought he would nickname me Nimfa, as he told me long ago, but doubts had changed his mind.

"*Yes dear*, for this reason I'd call you Lily, Lily! Do you like Lily?" he kept repeating with pleasure.

"Sure dear, I'm honored to be the lily of the valley" I accepted thinking about the meaning that this flower assumed in representing all the qualities that Freddie possessed: the sweetness, the return to happiness, the genuineness, the nobility of mind, the simplicity and loyalty. It was like wearing his way of being.

The coincidences were not accidental. Some time ago I bought a painting with a flower, not knowing it was a lily of the valley. When one day I decided to see how lilies were made, I noticed the identity, so with a canvas marker I wrote the title of the song in yellow.

The soft lights of the lampshades did not allow me to see the heat and blush that pervaded my face. Freddie believed in me, but until then I hadn't been jonest with him. My conscience told me that the long-awaited moment had arrived.

When David and Sonia went out to smoke, and I remained face to face with Freddie, I took the opportunity to tell him that it wasn't true that *"Lily doesn't know"*, on the contrary...I was aware of many things that he should have known. I was reminded again of that scene of Freddie who continued to record video clips despite his illness, and at one point he asked Rudi Dolezal *"Are you ready?"*. At the moment I had to ask him that question.

"Yes dear, I was waiting for this moment", he said taking a long drag on his cigarette, to then emit the smoke that clouded the space that divided us. "Oh dear, I'm always quick to guess. I'm smart, what should I do..."

Although he tried to be ironic, in his voice I perceived curiosity comnined with a little anguish. When the air became transparent again, and I managed to see his eyes staring at mine, I began my speech, which I had often tried to memorize so as not to make a mistake and not to leave out a single detail.

"Freddie! I'll try to be honest with you all the way" and I took his hand in mine.

He listened attentively to me, continuing to smoke. I swallowed hard. The moment I had been looking and waiting for had arrived. I took a deep breath and started with the clue from the first time:

"Freddie, do you remember that statue you saw on your keychain last year in Munich?" he nodded. "It really exists. It was officially inaugurated on November 25, 1996 in Montreux, in the presence of your parents and your sister. There were also the other three Queen and Montserrat Caballè, your faithful Phoebe who often comes back to visit you in the square in front of the lake where they put it down."

After these words the silence was intense, but our souls were noisy. We stood still waiting for Freddie to assimilate the true meaning of those words. I was breathing hard, but he motioned me to continue and I resumed my speech with a sigh of relief.

"Another statue of you was in the lobby of the Dominion Theater, and Roger took it to his house. But there are more than 300 of them worldwide."

"How do you know what happened in the future if we are still in the present?" he said, intrigued even more by my first confession.

"Duty. The desire to let you know, and above all to get to know you, sent me back in time."

But how could I tell him that he was no longer physically among us? I had to tell him the right way. I had to tell him it was like it, and more.

He looked into my eyes with the amazament of someone who wants a reasonable answer. But the concept became abstract and I didn't even find the courage to continue talking for fear of making him feel bad.

But I owed it to him and to all the fans who every time expressed the desire for an otherworldly contact with him, to make him understand that we were still there. I gathered my strength and decided to continue:

"When you took the other trip, John, Brian and Roger felt such great pain that they decided to take a break, to reflect on their future. But on April 20, 1992 they organized a concert called the *Freddie Mercury Tribute Concert*, right at Wembley Stadium".

His gaze, buried in mine, spoke more than a thousand words.

"By *the other trip* you mean…?"

With great regret I shook my head in approval. Freddie surprised me by not looking particularly rehearsed, as if he knew...

"*I'm sorry*, dear."

"Oh don't worry! Go on" he said eager to know more.

"Many international artists attended, including Tony Iommi, Metallica, Guns N' Roses, David Bowie, Roger Daltrey, Robert Plant, George Michael, Annie Lennox, Liza Minnelli, Extreme, Def Leppard, Zucchero Fornaciari and Elton John."

"My Sharon…" his voice was sweet.

"The concert was watched on television by over a billion people. In addition to being an extraordinart event, it called the world's attention to one disease in particular."

I didn't have the courage to pronounce the word AIDS, but he immediately understood. Maybe because he had some doubts or a premonition, even if sometimes what happens to others seems so far away from us. He interrupted me to tell that, when he was down with David, he had heard the sound of the piano and had come upstairs. Hearing Tom's meowing he'd found in his room, he'd gone to get it, and there he'd noticed the clock with the luminous face on top of the bedside table. Being connected to my cell phone, every message was visible on both displays. Freddie had looked closely after the sound and had seen the notification of a message that had reached me from a fan, exactly on May 23, 2021, in which it was written:

"*46 years since its release,* Bohemian Rhapsody *has been awarded diamond disc in the United States.*"

"*I do not understand your language.* I got curious reading the title of the song. Could you tell me the full translation, dear?"

I told him that at the end of March 2021, *Boh Rhap* was certified diamond in the United States for having exceeded 10 million copies sold among physical format download and streaming, and that I would then explain the meaning of the latter two words better.

"Then it was really true when you told me you were from the future."

I nodded without saying a word.

"Tell me again!" he asked, impatient to know everything.

"Do you want to know what Brian said when he found out?" I asked him.

He shook his head slightly in agreement.

"He made this statement: *this is incredible news. At times like this I have to pinch myself to make sure it's all real. It goes beyond all the dreams we had. A huge thank you to everyone who has believed in us over the years.* Brian is now 73, Roger 71 and John 69. You would have been 75, but you said you had no aspirations of living to be 70...that would be so boring..."

And he continued: "And I also said: *If I were to die tomorrow, I wouldn't worry. I've had everything from life.*"

In his voice he could hear the confirmation of his questions, awareness and acceptance in the most serene way possible.

"Tell me, what are those three doing without me?" he asked me about the other Queen.

"When they got over your loss the three remaining members got together, considering making one last album under the Queen name, using some vocals you had already recorded. Afterwards Brian and Roger did not stop playing, however John's last appearance with the rest of the band dates back to January 17, 1997, at the *Ballet for Life - Music by Queen & Mozart* held in Paris."

"John! *My friend...*". I had never seen Freddie so melancholy.

"*Please*, Freddie! Get the watch!" I invited him, and he whipped it out of his pocket in an instant. I showed him at the same time from my phone how to surf the internet and use it to read anything that interested him.

"Navigate? Oh dear, I'm not a good swimmer" he made one of his jokes, accompanied by the gesture of the hand going down.

"But I'll give you the donut to stay afloat" I retorted smiling to lighten those moments.

Even in those delicate and impactful moments, Freddie managed to be himself, ironic and funny. Having broken the tension of the moment, I found the strength to continue.

"Come, I'll show you where to enter the keyword. Try!" I told him and he wrote *"Queen"*.

He couldn't write another name. Queen as Her Royal Highness. He was Queen. He had thought of that name for the band and he had to see with his own eye that Queen had remained such, and he himself immortal. He picked up my phone to read better, when a video of Brian playing guitar in his house played.

"Sometimes he does it directly from social media" said Sonia who rad recently joined us.

Without taking his eyes off the screen he asked: "Social? What are they?". Sonia tried to explain in a simple way, but the concept seemed so absurd to him, thinking of connecting, being seen or being in real time contact with fans, that he struggled to understand this novelty.

"Brian's hair is white, but the cut has remained the same. Oh my old Bri!" he exclaimed in astonishment.

Surely it was strange to see him aged. Impatiently he wanted to see the other two. "Roger is fine, a little more chubby. It still sounds loud." And when he saw John strolling in Greenwich Park he reached out to "touch" him from the screen. "Maybe he's going to get his bass", he said softly.

"Surely at his house he plays it for his six children and grandchildren" I reinforced so as not to lead him to think otherwise. In the end we all remember Deacon with his instrument in hand. Freddie wanted it that way too.

I saw a little displeasure on his face and to alleviate this bad feeling, I flattered him: Instead you, Freddie, stayed *forever young*."

"Keep reading!" he almost gave me an order.

"Summer 1992, EMI released *Live at Wembley '86*, the complete edition of 1986 Wembley concert, which was part of the Magic Tour. *Made in Heaven was released in 1995,* broughing Queen back to the top of the sales charts. The opening track, *It's a Beautiful Day*, a piano solo accompanied by Mercury's only vocals, is the most exemplary track of the album, conceived as a celebratory record of Queen's past years, which contained Mercury's last vocal tracks, such as *You Don't Fool Me, A Winter's Tale and Mother Love*."

"*It's beautiful. Yeah!* Another album" he said satisfied.

"January 5, 1998. The three remaining members of Queen, record a song dedicated to Freddie Mercury, entitled *No One But You*."

He started listening to it...

"Freddie! You are their angel who has reached heaven."

And he continued: "And life goes on...together with the show."

No one had ever seen him cry, and even in this delicate moment, just to hide his emotion, I continued reading.

"In 2002, a musical based on the songs of Queen, entitled *We Will Rock You*, opened at the Dominion Theater in London. The musical was written by English author and screenwriter Ben Elton, in collaboration with May and Roger, and produced by Robert De Niro."

While scrolling the internet pages, *Living on My Own* remix appeared. He began to listen to it by moving his hand to the rhythm and said: *"Wow, how great!"*

"You told Jim Beach to do what he wanted with your music, without making you boring. And he did. Instead, the song *Barcelona* has been adapted for an eighty-piece orchestra. Extremely beautiful. I'll let you listen to it later."

He shook his head happily and I continued reading.

"In 2007 two polls conducted by the BBC declared Queen the best British band of all time. On November 24, 2009, a plaque was placed in Feltham, near the house where Mercury and his family had moved upon their arrival in England in 1964; also a star was installed in Feltham High Street, in memory of the singer's successes, at the inauguration of which Jer Bulsara and Brian May were present.

In September 2010, a poll of rock fans named Mercury *Greatest Rock Legend of All Time*, ahead of Elvis Presley, David Bowie, Jon Bon Jovi, Jimi Hendrix and Ozzy Osbourne."

"More than Jimi Hendrix!?" he asked incredulously.

"You realize? You are the only artist who has surpassed his idol" I congratulated. "And not only. Three years ago in BBC Radio 2's *Greatest British Band of All Time* pool, Queen overtook the Beatles, leaving behind the Rolling Stone, Oasis and Take That. Thousands of spectators voted, judging the groups for music, lyrics, concerts and originality. You said you didn't want to be a star, you wanted to be a legend, and you became one."

"And you have become our idol, since November 2018 when the film about your life, *Bohemian Rhapsody*, was released, and it is from there that we began to get to know you better and to become your avid fans" Sonia intervened again.

"A film about me? I'm so curious to see it."

"The actor Rami Malek played you brilliantly. I'll show you one day", she promised. "Brian says you would have loved it".

"Ah, if he says so...Brian knows me very well".

"The film brought Queen back to the world scene, and it is thanks to this that the number of fans of the new generation has increased."

"And those boring paparazzi, they couldn't blame me anymore. I've always fucked them."

"Forget them. Real writers and real journalists know what to write. We see several documentaries on TV and we still hear Queen's songs on various broadcasts and on the radio. Some of the people who knew you well have written many books about you and it is thanks to them that we, the fans, know everything about your life."

"Have they written or will they write?"

"It doesn't matter if they have or will. The time to know all this is now."

He looked at me quite convinced, then added:

"Paul told me last year that Jim had written a book about us". He was referring to the book he had confiscated from me. "Haha, Jim, can you imagine that? Of course, dear ones, I have stopped believing in that manipulator."

"It is the truth. So many people who were close to you have written books about you."

The cracking of the relationship with Prenter was clear. I just told him to be careful of him. I didn't want to touch the subject anymore and I passed over it by glancing at Sonia, who understood me immediately and continued:

"Rudi and I emailed a TV newsroom so they would show more coverage about you and Queen."

"E-mail?" he made a strange face.

"Yes, a kind of letter that you write on your computer and send over the internet."

I wasn't sure he understood all that future technology terminology in such a short amount of time. Sonia kept talking and my look of thanks for supporting me and sharing a difficult but satisfying moment like this, came to him like never before.

"Come closer! Look" she wanted to show him what he would do in the following years. "You will sing with Montserrat Caballè."

"No...that's impossible" he replied, but his eyes sparkled at the prospect of singing with his favorite soprano.

"You will do great things as you have done so far. Stay that way, genuine and sincere, just like you shine through in your songs."

His heart was full of joy and pain at the same time, but ours was full of him.

"And Mary? And Jim?" he kept asking.

"After a few years, Jim joined you to arrange the garden of your paradise... Instead Mary looked after and took care of everything. I'm sure she never forgot you."

He was surprised more than I thought to discover so many things together. Seeing him a little melancholy, Sonia continued to tell other events.

"Freddie! Do you remember the *Queen International Fan Club*, founded in 1973 in London?"

"*Yes, I remember*, and I will never forget the fans."

"In 2004 it was recognized by the Guinness Book of World Records as the longest lasting fan club in the world. It means that your fans have never stopped listening to your voice and remembering you with love and dedication every single day. We have a place where we all get together from all over the world to talk about you and Queen, remembering concerts, the reliease of a single song or just posting your photos from the very beginning. Read the comments...Look! There is that of Ilaria, Giovanna, Cris, Valerio, Sabrina, Serena, Antonella, Simona, Saren, Venere, Anna, Francesco, Sara, Lorella, Katia Natasha, Linda, Ricky, Andrea, Irene, Serenella, Emmy, Matina, Federica, Laura and many others who supported your mother, constantly sending letters to let her know how important your music was to them. Not knowing the right address, they wrote *To Freddie Mercury's mother, England*. And the Royal Mail delivered them right away. Surely mom Jer shared them with your father and sister."

I decided to remove that veil of sadness by shifting his attention.

"Come a little closer Freddie, I'll show you a backstage shot!"

Rudi and Peter appeared on the screen together.

"But look at these two having fun without me," he said, bringing his face closer to the screen.

"However, every year in Montreux, on the first weekend of September, many of your fans gather in Switzerland to participate in *Freddie Celebration Days*" I spoke again.

"I'm proud of you and of all my fans" he was moved.

"A star and a rose bear your name. You are everything to us fans. Freddie, you are our satellite, which revolves around us incessantly, and we are the inhabitants of the planet Mercury, we are the ones closest to you, our sun, and no one can turn you off because the energy you emanate permeates and warms each of us."

"I will turn the wait into an uninterrupted work to leave the fans with as many songs as possible."

He opened his arms and wrapped us warmly in a strong mutual embrace.

"You and us" we whispered to him. He squeezed us even tighter and said: *"Thank you!"*

"*We love you Freddie.* All the fans love you". His arms were still around us. "Now what are you going to do?"

"In the meantime, I'm giving myself a short but wonderful holiday in Japan. Time waits for no one."

***

A fan writes on the bulletin board: *"Hello group, simple question but as always I hope appetizing. What would you ask Freddie when you find him in front of you? I'll have my say after you."*

These are some of the answers:

"You have given meaning to my life, many times you have saved it. Thank you for existing Freddie."

"I would hug him tightly saying: You are great!*"*

"I would ask him if he would do everything the same again in his life and if he was happy."

"Can I hug you? You gave me so much, even though I didn't know you."

"How are you Freddie...how are you really?"

"I would ask him to let me hear everything he would have composed so far, if he hadn't flown away from us."

"Just thank you for the wonderful time I had with your songs, and happy to see you again."

"I think a stumble of meaningless words would come out, because the emotion would be so great."

"Lucky you who can talk in front of him."

"I would hug him to smell his perfume, his heartbeat, in certain moments words are not needed."

***

Is this the real life?
Is this just fantasy?
Any way the wind blows
Nothing really matters to me
Bohemian Rhapsody (Queen, October 31, 1975)

THE ANNIVERSARIES

CHRISTMAS

When Christmas arrives, a veil of nostalgia and melancholy spreads over every face, and the memory of that precise event comes alive more than ever.

Freddie was of the Zoroastrian religion, even if not practicing, but he really liked celebrating Christmas. As a child, together with his family he usually went to the ancient Zoroastrian Fire Temple, where events and birthdays took place, some of which Freddie celebrated right there.

On December 21, Zoroastrians celebrate the night of the birth of their sun deity, Mitra. The bond between Rome and Persia gave rise to the Christian feast of Christmas, as Christianity was recognized as the state religion in 380. Zoroastrians, when they noticed that Christians were tied to this feast, decided to make it official, celebrating it on last day of the festival for the birth of the deity of light. Maybe because Christmas represents the link between the two religions better than any other day holiday. Reading a bit of history, this question arose spontaneously, but even if it weren't so, I am of the opinion that everyone is free to celebrate whatever they want.

Freddie wrote *Jesus* and *Mustapha* both with a complete religious characterization, respectively Christian and Muslim, because he was of the opinion that everyone should follow the right religion for them. This message of peace is still useful today.

You enjoyed decorating the tree and putting gifts under it. Christmas for you was a party where you gathered friends, with whom you sang Christmas carols on the eve. You didn't like the idea that someone could be left alone, so you invited everyone, showing boundless hospitality and a festive spirit. Your generosity was unparalleled: you knew your friends and their preferences well, and it took you time to find the right gift for them, always accompanied by a greeting card that you personally wrote and signed. Your strong taste for beauty came out above all in decorating the house with floral arrangements and the ever-present Christmas tree.

The gesture he made on Boxing Day, a month after his death, for his dear friend Elton John, is unprecedented. Through their mutual friend, Tony King, he sent him home a watercolor entitled *Boys Bathing*, by his favorite painter Henry Scott Tuke. It blown me away to the point of leaving me speechless. Even accompanied by a written note: *"Dear Sharon, I saw it at an auction and thought you might like it. I love you"*, signed Melina. Your concept of friendship was beyond life, again demostrating what an amazing and selfless person you were. And we can only take an example from you.

With the altruism that characterized you, every Christmas, knowing that the patients of the AIDS department could not have their loved ones close by, you offered a great Christmas Eve dinner, giving them a small moment of happiness.

***

It's Christmas 2020 and my tree is dedicated to Queen's career. On each branch there is a record cover and live images. There are photos of Freddie and those of John, Roger, and Brian who act as a tip together with the red *Flash* symbol, his most significant silhouette with a raised fist made with yellow lenci cloth, next to a star of the same color, then a sort of "nativity scene" with an angel with a guitar and cats, ducks and koi carp in the background, above a blue surface with the same color of the lights that bring out the color of the lake, a 2002 Harrods ball, surprisingly jumped out I can't say where, and invariably your photo, the *Bicycle Race* bike, *Boh Rhap's music box* and a train similar to the one in *Breakthru,* the train of my turning point, the one that passes only once and that I took without thinking about it twice, it was enough just for me to say to myself: "Come into my life. It's an artificial paradise".

This is how fans remember Freddie as Christmas approaches.

"It is said to be the most beautiful night of the year. After the frantic rush for gifts, food to cook, people to greet, we stop. We sit on the sofa, look at the lighted Christmas tree, think. And even if not everything in life goes your way, you realize that it's not so bad after all. There are riches that we often dont't see, but are close to us: our loved ones, friends (even four-legged ones), the sun and stars, music. Freddie saw all these things and felt serenity. Merry Christmas!"

"Even this Christmas has passed, with its hugs, gifts, smiles and kisses. And you, Freddie, will have noticed that in each of our homes, in one way or another, you were present."

Because it's Christmas
Yes, it's Christmas
Thank God, it's Christmas
For one night
Thank God It's Christmas (Queen, 1984)

***

VALENTINE'S DAY

Valentine's Day is the celebration dedicated to love, and Freddie was in love with love. He dedicated many songs to this beautiful feeling. He's done it since the inception of Queen. Constantly looking for the most attractive emotion, he sang about the love that breaks your heart and ruins your heart rate, that leaves you breathless and just won't sit still, that can play with your emotions and causes you pain, the one that doesn't pay the bills nor take reservations or even justify, the strongest love, the love that conquers all, the love that walks tall, the love that crosses the walls.

He, born to love but also to be loved, has never stopped asking to be loved as if there were no tomorrow. Always looking for that real emotion, even when he knew that February 14, 1991 could be his last Valentine's Day, Freddie gave Jim a gift anyway. He was trying to give rather than receive. It is no coincidence that the word *Love* appears in the verses of almost all of his songs. The great ability to inspire love and affection was seen in all who knew him. *Notre Bijou*, we are destined to love him forever, and your *Love of My Life* will be a hymn to true love over the centuries.

***

A fan says: *"Lucky whoever spent 45 Valentine's Day with you."*

And yet another: *"Happy Valentine's Dat to all and happy Valentine's Day to you, sweet Freddie, who were love personified. If today, after so many years, I slowly begin to appreciate this day again despite being alone, if I'm slowly starting to believe in love again, it's only thanks to you."*

> *I can serenade and gently play*
> *On your heart strings*
> *Be your Valentino just for you*
> *Good Old-Fashioned Lover Boy* (Queen, 1977)

Freddie has expressed the words love and life in almost all the songs composed by him, but also those in collaboration with the band and in solo albums. The liason between the two concepts is often seen in the same song. Painstakingly, as only a devoted fan could, I read all the lyrics of the songs, to find the verses.

LOVE
1- Seaside Rendez-Vous - I love you madly
2- Love of My Life - Love of my life don't leave me
3- Pain Is So Close to Pleausure - So in love but love had
4- Friends Will Be Friends - It's not easy love
5- Princes of The Universe - I'm here for your love
6- All God's People - Love and be free
7- Delilah - I love you
8- The Hit Man - I'm gonna kill for you love
9- Keep Passing the Open Windows - Love is all you need
10- Play the Game - is fall in love - Everybody play the game of love
11- Crazy Little Thing Called Love
12- Get Down, Make Love
13- Mother Love
14- I Was Born to Love You
15- My Baby Does Me - My baby loves me
16- You Take My Breath Away - You've captured my love
17- The Millionaire Waltz - Bring out the charge of the love brigade, Come back to me of my love
18- Somebody to Love - Can anybody find me somebody to love
19- Good Old-Fashioned Lover Boy - I love you
20- Jealousy - Oh to fall in my love
21- Funny How Love Is - I you gotta make love do it everywhere
22- Love Kills
23- Love Me Like There's No Tomorrow
24- My Love Is Dangerous
25- Thank God It's Christmas- Oh, my love, we've had our share of tears

LIFE
1-Love of My Life
2- Bohemian Rapsody - Is this the real life
3-Pain Is So Close to Pleasure- together all your life

4- *Friend Will Be Friends - When you're through with life*
5- *Don't Cry So Hard - Is this the life for me*
6- *Ride the Wild Wind Live - Life on the razors edge*
7- *These Are the Days of Your Lives - The rest of my life's been*
8- *The Hit Man - I want your life*
9- *Keep Passing the Open Windows - This is the only life for me*
10- *This Is the World We Created - Waiting for life to so by*
11- *Play the Game -This is your life*
12- *Let Me Live - Why don't you take another little piece of my life*
13- *Mother Love - To make me feel my life is heading somewhere*
14- *My Life Has Been Saved*
15- *I Was Born to Love You - Every single day of my life*
16- *Khashoggi's Ship - The best years of my life are like a supernova*
17- *I Want It All - So much to do in one life time*
18- *The Invisible Man - And I'm in your life*
19- *Breakthru - A new life is born*
20- *Rain Must Fall - Life is so exciting*
21- *Scandal - It's only a life to be twisted and broken*
22- *Was It All Worth It - What is there left for me to do in this life*
22- *You Take My Breath Away - Changed my life*
23- *Fat Bottomed Girls -But I knew life before I left my nursey*
24- *In the Laps of the Gods - I live my life for you*
25- *Life Is Real*
26- *Cool Cat - Making such a dead of life*
27- *Nevermore - There's no living in my life anymore*
28- *The March of The Black Queen - You've never seen nothing like it no never in your life*
29- *Seven Seas of Rhye - Sister – I live and life for you*

30- The Fallen Priest - I life of sacrifice controlled me (album solista)
31- The Golden Boy - I love you for you silence (album solista)
32- Man Mad Paradise - come into my life (album solista)
33- There Must Be More to Life Than This

The two substantial words that express your *love for life* teach us that it must be lived to the end, without remorse and without regrets.

***

ANNIVERSARY OF DEATH

In general I don't like remembering the day of his death, because it makes me feel sad, and I prefer to avoid the negative emotions it gives me. I could never remember the day Freddie disappeared as I didn't experience it first hand, but I have seen the heartbreaking videos from the time. In an interview, Freddie points up with his finger and says: "He watches over me".

And you watch over us. I'm not afraid of death and you gave me this courage. Reaching you will be like being reborn somewhere else near you and close to my loved ones. You will be the inhabitant of my heart until I come to you.

November 24, 2020

Someone rang the intercom and I didn't have time to see who it was when I found a package for me on the stairs. I was convinced I'd find a little box in the mailbox, because I was waiting for a keychain with a picture of Freddie from one of the girls I had bonded with the most, instead I found a large box with *Queen Flora* written on it. Ironically I thought that the keyhole wasn't that big or maybe they were just wrong, however I took it up to the house and tried to figure out who had sent it, but the sender's name was missing. As the television remembered Freddie with a series of songs, I opened it and gasped to see my favorite flowers and was moved by the sight of twelve red roses that very day. Usually on the day of the disappearance of people dear to me I try to occupy the time so as not to remember that bad moment. Those tears that I had been holding back all day poured down me like torrential rain. I was waiting for an answer that I found in this sentence: *Freddie not only unites in friendship, but also creates sisterhood and has incredible strength in uniting people.* Despite the pain we feel as fans, we manage to transform into strength even in this particular moment, and the voice of our Highlander helps us do it.

***

All fans pay tribute to Freddie on this sad day and I think it's only right to describe their way of commemorating him.

"Do you hear us, Freddie? We always talk about you, listen to your music, let your heavenly voice fill our souls. We are your audience, and we love you. We will never forget you, you are always with us."

"He doesn't want us to be sad on November 24th. As the song says, The Show Must Go On. *He will always be with us wherever we are. He gave us his voice and his records, which are like rare pearls for us. On the 24th we must be one family to be happy and listen to his songs forever."*

"I write today because tomorrow I will give way to silence. November 24, 1991. They were all left without their own voice (for dismay) and without a voice (his). Today dismay seizes us at times, but mitigated by the awareness that his voice will always remain to keep us company and to shine, intense, warm, passionate, in everyone's life forever. It is a human consolation, unfortunately, because we are all destined to die. However, great love (in this specific case represented by music and vocal interpretation), overcomes the barriers of time and the limit of the transience of the body. Thank you Freddie, your life and your giving of yourself to music and for music has represented for all of us and for all future generations a true miracle of survival, inspiration, expression and sharing."

"29 years. An eternity. Yet it doesn't seem like a single day has passed. You guessed it when you said that you would not become a star, but a legend...you were right. Everything is as you left it. And who knows, I want to think that maybe you are having a good time somewhere, with

your will to live my dear Freddie, lover of life, singer of songs."

"Not everyone understands that you love him beyond his death."

"Because deep down you never died. Your death was a detail. An existence like yours has its destiny sealed. You could never age like ordinary mortals and you didn't die, you just handed yourself over the eternity. Today is a sad day, it's true, but it's the day you entered our lives and became ours forever. Hi Fred, wherever you are."

***

BIRTHDAY

"I'm not worried about being younger or older, I just want to live life to the fullest by doing wonderful things."

Freddie Mercury – Words and thoughts

September 5, 2020

That blessed September 5, 1946, mom Jer gave birth to a child with a beautiful smile, destined to become responsible for the well-being of many people who still follow this *enfant prodige* today with so much dedication and love.

Like every year there are celebrations dedicated to our star, such as the *Freddie Mercury Birthday Party at* Montreux in Switzerland. The themes of the party are different every year. This year I read that it is *The Great Pretender*, with the pink and black colors of Freddie's stage costume in the video clip. Fans organize especially for his birthday, a real coming and going of people from all over the world. Instead the various Hard Rock Cafè, in addition to the celebrations, also organize fundraising for the Mercury Phoenix Trust, to support research against AIDS and HIV.

Since the mid-80s in particular, Freddie loved to celebrate his birthdays in an exaggerated way, but even before he knew how to do it with gusto. Curious I go to see the videos of how Freddie celebrated his birthdays.

September 5, 1977.

His 31st birthday. There are Mary, Roger, Elton John and other famous people, thousands of flowers decorate the establishment from top to bottom. The taste for beauty was part of Freddie's way of being.

The most excessive seems to be Ibiza 1987, forty-first birthday, 80 guests with a plane from London at their disposal. After a breakdown, they manage to land with one engine. Another inconvenience happens during the evening. The banners catch fire following an irresponsible behavior of a girl, and furthermore only a mass of marzipan and decorations remains of the beautiful Gaudì-style cake, but those around him immediately make a huge tart. The fun was certainly not lacking, but Freddie took it a bit. Black and gold balloons, fireworks and a thousand people, this is how Pike's lived that September 5th and still today remembers the singer in the first week of September.

Then comes that of September 1990 in which the excess is reduced. The clear signs of the disease are visible, but this does not prevent him from celebrating in his beloved Garden Lodge, all around a huge table and, as always, on his right, Mary. Then there's Jim, Peter, Dave Clark. Freddie is very elegant in his blue tuxedo.

You would have turned 74 and you would have been stratospheric all the same, because you were as much terrestrial as you were space. You belonged to the universe, and it made sure that you lived part of your life close to your loved ones and your fans, and the other part a little further away, but now you were inside each of us, and we would never let you go.

At Garden Lodge a little girl wrote a letter and placed it in front of the door full of bouquests, while a young girl sang in the middle of the street *Love of My Life,* the most beautiful love song ever. I shivered and moved, but I didn't want to cry anymore on your birthday. Other fans sat along the sidewalk. They stayed there until the sun sank below the horizon line and gave way to the sunset, which slowly faded, its colors giving way to darkness that greeted this unusual day. Suddenly your beloved house lit up with a light of hope that killed me with nostalgia. A war, light that lit the atmosphere. In a fraction of a second I thought you were there celebrating with so many guests, as only you know how to do. I moved closer to the screen to look better in an attempt to catch a sign, a shadow, the notes of a melody, the meow of a cat... *or maybe it was Mary.*

My thoughts inevitably went to her, always present by his side, with her ever-present smile and sweet gaze towards him, with her support, her reserve and elegance, ready to accept everything for the love she felt for him. She will have suffered in silence after his disappearance, away from the spotlight, from everyone, but close to her children who will surely remember the jokes and gifts that Uncle Freddie gave them. Even though she no longer lived at Garden Lodge, I imagined her taking refuge there from time to time, where every remaining object reminded her of a special day, a birthday, a Christmas. Everything reminded her of him and his unconditional love which remained in the air and she would go and breathe it in small doses every now and then like a breath of life. Who knows how much she missed him. Who better than her knew him so well? It is no coincidence that Freddie entrusted his ashes to Mary, perhaps saying these words: *"I love being free. I want to be free like the air. I think I've gotten too used to it."*

In any case, I'm sure she gets the affection we feel for you, Freddie, even after so long. I truly hope that she can read how much we adore you, and that void that created your only love can be filled, at least a little, with that of your wild fans, those who remember your extraordinary and unique love on earth, those that not a day goes by without remembering you, because for us too, what we feel for you is unconditional love.

In an interview I heard recently, but which should have been released years ago Mary says:

"It took me a long time to really fall in love with this man, but when it happened, I just couldn't walk away from him. His pain became my pain, his joy became my joy. I was able to almost look into him and what I saw was a treasure trove of beauty."

And addressing the fans she continues:

"I think the same thing is happening to a few million people as well. That's why I think fans continue to feel for him. They've seen that beauty, they've seen the fun, they've seen all aspects of Freddie's personality. They too fell in love with him. A beautiful thing."

Anyone like me who has experienced this beautiful feeling can be found in Mary's words. A feeling that accompanies you every moment, fills your soul, drives you as only love can do and on special days it stands out more, incredibly, setting in motion a search mechanism for events to be able to say "Happy birthday", perhaps from a place more experienced by you, where I feel closer to you and where I prefer to think of you as immortal and still at the age of 45.

***

Fan comments on this special day are truly touching.

"Today is a special day. On this day 74 years ago you were born. There are no words to describe what you mean to us, what you mean to me. Your passion, your extraordinary voice, your way of enchanting everyone when you performed on stage, your generosity, your

sensitivity, your determination, your genius. You are and will always be in our hearts because legends never die! Happy birthday Freddie wherever you are! + 74."

"There will never again be anyone in the world like you. Greetings my breath."

"Happy birthday Freddie, you are a special person, I miss you so much. Without your songs my life would not exist."

"Every time September 5th approaches, it feels like I'm about to celebrate a family member's birthday. I have anxiety like when I prepare my children's party, because even if Freddie has been missing for the past 29 years, for me it is as if he were still alive, so it is very necessary to celebrate the birth of a legend."

***

September 4, 2021, CELEBRATION DAY MONTREUX, Freddie's 75th anniversary

I returned to Montreux just for the anniversary of Freddie's birthday. A very pleasant car journey with other fans (Sonia, Francesco, Luca, Annarita) and Giuseppe and Blendi who were already waiting for us there, listening to Queen's repertoire all the way. While we were listening to *Mother Love,* I saw a tear escape from Sonia, which she quickly wiped away with a smile, even if I had time to get emotional. This is pure love for Freddie.

But it was *We Are The Champions* that acted as a soundtrack in the streets of Montreux, which seen from above was something exceptional. In the Place du Marchè the festivities had begun two days earlier. Freddie's voice filled the square packed with people coming from all over the world for him.

A talented internationally renowned Russian pianist, Peter A, played Queen songs on the piano in an extraordinary manner, and the fans sang in chorus. One of the best I've seen so far, after Freddie of course. Subsequently, a well-prepared choir of boys directed by an orchestra conductor, enthusiastically sang various songs, while Queen simulated their movements, a young singer sang *The Show Must Go On*, but what struck me most was a 10-year-old girl who knew all the songs by heart, and danced in front of everyone. Surely she will be one of the many who will inherit a passion from Queen as adults. And when another 40 years go by and we no longer say "Freddie Mercury would have turned 115 today", they will still be there in the square to remember him, to write one more thought on the notebook left on purpose next to the statue, as we did too, and above all to sing the timeless songs of the band that in those days had a large number of listeners on Spotify, beating the Beatles, Rolling Stones, Led Zeppelin and even Michael Jackson, and it is precisely as a sign of victory that Freddie's hand seems to touch the sun, shining even more, highlighting the yellow of the clothes worn by the fans. The focus captured the right moment. Freddie had the sun in his fist, so he decided to make those days radiant.

We couldn't wait to visit The Studio Experience, also because I had visited it in a hurry last time. Even Francesco, who had come here way back in 2006, when the studio hadn't yet become a museum, felt the need to go there right away.

Francesco knelt down to touch the memorial plaque where Freddie was last physically, and the emotional involvement came loud and clear to everyone else. We sat around the plaque to capture this emotional impact, which was worth a thousand words, because even though we had our heads lowered and our eyes fixed on his name, we could feel what we were feeling in that poignant moment. Silence accompanied us for almost the entire lakefront that we took to arrive at the magnificent apartment on the top floor of the residence in Territet. From what would be seen from below, the boys preferred to stay downstairs, while I decided to climb the numerous external stairs that took me exactly in front of the door. On the left the writing *Les Tourelles*. I felt sad in thinking that when Freddie came here he was not well, but nevertheless he made every effort to decorate it according to his tastes. As luck would have it, someone opened it telling me that it was private property and you couldn't enter, but realizing from the accent that its origin was also mine, I spoke to him in our language and he let me into the hall. I was able to take just two photos of this stately building. I went back down to tell the others, who thought it was a joke. In a way it was a twist of fate, which made me even happier.

We returned to the square where we found Rudi Dolezal. I approached to give him the book I created on Freddie's life as a gift. I introduced myself: "My pleasure, Rudi". He was surprised by both the common name and the production in PowerPoint, and asked me: "Did you do it yourself?". After leafing through it in a hurry, he complimented me: *"It's beautiful."*

"Thank you" I thanked him and asked for a signature, while he offered to take a picture. It was strange to think that I had had the opportunity to meet someone so close to Freddie. I would have asked him a lot of questions, but I didn't want to be intrusive.

September 5, 2021

I did the same the next day, on Freddie's birthday, with Peter Freestone. Giving it to them felt like giving it to Freddie. Unfortunately Peter, after telling us some anecdotes about Freddie's life, hurried away.

As for the ritual, I also left a heart hanging on Freddie's arm, along with other gifts scattered under the statue. The most awaited moment was that of the thanks and the three-tier cake with his image in the yellow jacket on it, and by chance I found myself near the workers who were carrying it. A crazy choir sang *Happy Birthday to You*, accompanied by applause.

Slowly darkness dominated the square which slowly empied, but it was still your day, Freddie, and we, to celebrate with a Moet Chandon and a bluetooth speaker, sat down at your feet, to toast one more year with you. It was a very dark night. This time your fist enclosed a star, because you had hidden the moon somewhere so as not to show the melancholy in our faces. You used to keep pranking us.

The next day we concluded our trip with a boat tour, from where we admired the statue from another perspective, the much loved Duck House, all of Montreux and the nearby villages, which filled our eyes with colors.

We left as acquaintances who shared a passion for Queen, and returned with the added value of friendship. It is no coincidence that *We Are the Champions* accompanied us from the beginning of this beautiful adventure, because we, together with you, Freddie, returned as champions. And Katia, who was unable to come with us, wrote her thoughts:

"The whole world is celebrating you my Queen. I will not become a star. I will become a legend. You have become. Your charisma has managed to outclass everything. Congratulations my Great Love!"

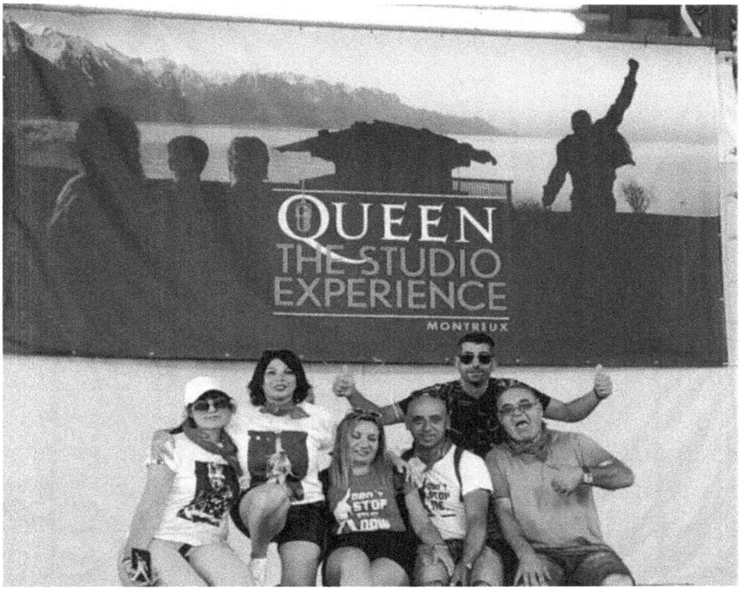
QUEEN
THE STUDIO
EXPERIENCE
MONTREUX

THE RETURN TO THE DUCK HOUSE

03-08 January 2022

The adventurous spirit of Alice in Wonderland prompted me to return for the second time to my center of the globe, to that where the red drop of the position is almost invisible, or in the house of the Queens of Hearts.

I climbed over the gate, and just like her when she remembered her cat left alone, as she descended into the well, I began to fall down the many lamp-lit stairs. At one point I stopped short, and my gaze was directed in a parallel line. Les Cornettes de Bise, Les Jumelles, Le Linleu and other mountains around had their peaks covered with the white veil of peace, which this time reigned among us. I landed softly on dry twigs and leaves and proceeded along a narrow passage that led to the main entrance. Before entering, I turned my head towards the huge garden. The trees had dropped their leaves, baring themselves. Surrender to replace. The nature-facing ducks welcomed me. They had remained motionless there waiting for me, sure of my return,

The Liddell sisters had reunited again.

"It's wonderful here" the youngest exclaimed happily, hugging me tightly.

Everything around us was fantastic and we were wonderful. The amazement in the eyes of my friends was identical to the one I had felt the first time I entered that house that had hosted Queen. Each time it was like stepping into the past. The board games were perfectly preserved: the Scrabble, just like the one exhibited at the Studio Experiences, the checkers, the wooden games. While those who had arrived before me were already playing, the first thing I did was go look for that notebook which from the outside looked like a book with a mice title, because I didn't exactly remember the thought I had left the first time I entered the Duck House. So I looked for it where I had left it, in the library, but it wasn't there. I hadn't thought about taking a picture before leaving, and this increased my curiosity, because I didn't exactly remember the words I had written in a hurry. I found it in the hall, on a cabinet. Among other dedications that had been added later, I recognized mine:

"Hello Freddie! I came to see you in your home. I couldn't feel you any closer than this. I woke up with your songs, imagining you in every corner. I felt your presence. You are here with me. I will come back...Rudi"

A promise unconsciously kept. The flames of the fireplace warmed our cheerful souls. From the huge speakers, the voices of Luca, Sonia and Francesco singing Queen's songs at karaoke underlined why we were there, just to experience our band to the fullest. After dinner, I suggested that we play a little game. Think about who you would dedicate the writing in the wrapper of a chocolate to before discarding it. Who indicated the partner, who a friend, who the team of the heart and who, like me, Freddie. Never have sentences been so spot on, but mine left me speechless to the point of moving me.

"As I saw you, I feel in love."

The next day was a splendid day. Our preparations for the *Yellow Party* started early in the morning. Beppe was always the firts to get up and prepare breakfast for everyone, and wasted no time in getting busy because the menu of the day had to be strictly yellow: saffron risotto, polenta, peperonata, turmeric bread, corn paste, skewers of Emmenthal cheese and yellow cherry tomatoes stuffed into winter melon, limoncello, citron, then pineapple, bananas that someone put on their heads and we knew why, we were mad with joy.

Freddie liked themed parties, and we were working like him to make it unforgettable. Above the yellow passepartouts, his name and a large-format *Eeeeooo* lined the walls.

Tablecloths and cutlery in a perfect match, just like the clothes we wore. Sonia and Annarita made some biscuits. Pigotta and I took care of setting up the environment with yellow sheets, blankets with Freddie's image, flowers, our gifts to be exchanged wrapped in the same color. One in particular was well exposed. Beppe, with his golden hands, had reproduced the wooden house in miniature.

The sun's rays entered through the huge windows, multiplying its own shades. To give more vitality to the organized event, Gabriel (13 years old), our mascot, took care of inflating the yellow balloons and occasionally popping them to play a joke. Like the Knave of Hearts, he occasionally came to steal the cat biscuits.

Yeah, children are fantasising
Grown-ups are standin' by
What a super feeling

A Winter's Tale (Queen)

At the end of the party I decided to surprise my friends. I secretly wore the cape, the king's crown and a mask with Freddie's face and with the complicity of Pigotta, who started *God Save the Queen*, I thanked them for participating. Silence reigned for a moment, which ended in a final applause.

There were no words to describe that feeling, stronger and stronger and that each of us perceived differently. There were those who withdrew to seek a more personal and close contact with Freddie, as in the case of Pigotta, who already said to me from the first evening:

"You didn't realize it, but I was looking out the window in Freddie's room for 20 minutes, while all of you were in the hall. I called him and I perceived him in that corner over there" pointing in the red wall to a corner next to an antique lampshade. I took her statement lightly, smiled at her and walked down the long, narrow corridor, shaking my head in disbelief. It was the second time I'd slept in that room, but I hadn't had any visions or anything, just some beautiful abstract sensations.

That same night, Pigotta came to us saying that she could hear breathing in her room. I tried to reassure her by telling that it was the small waves of the lake banging on the reinforced concrete, when Sonia added:

"Every time I pass in front of Pigotta's room (the first to be clear), I feel an unease mixed with fear for something I feel."

I began to wonder if there was anything true or if sometimes fantasy takes over, until another episode happened the next day. We were in full preparation for the party. In the kitchen, Pigotta was washing the dishes, I had just approached the stove and Sonia, who was standing between the yellow wall on the left and the table on the right, was talking to Beppe, when she suddenly interrupted the conversation, going out the door into unusual way, as it following someone, I saw her a little shaken, contrary to her calm nature. I walked up behind her and when she turned she took me aside. We went to Freddie's room, as well as ours, and she started telling me:

"I saw a black cat with a white spot on its face." Her breathing quickened. From her seriousness, I knew she was telling me the truth. "It was as if it had come out of Pigotta's leg (who was next to her). I followed it out of the corner of my eye without interrupting that moment. The cat walked calmly towards the living room. Then it disappeared..."

I looked at her petrified, trying to understand, but I had no questions to ask her, because I blindly believed in her and in what she was telling me.

It was not lying over the fireplace like the Cheshire Cat, not even on a tree, and it did not say *"That way lives the Mad Hatter"*. I don't know why, but instinctively I just said to her:

"It's Milo", one of Freddie's cats.

Although I remembered its colors very well, we immediately searched the internet for the details. As soon as she saw the picture, Sonia affirmed that it was it and I could not help but support and comfort her, even if after a few minutes that she had made it clear she said that this episode had given her so much serenity. Coincidentally she had brought along a towel with a picture of Freddie with his cats on a leash.

In the following days, we tried to face these signals with irony, even if they increased. Luca, who had chosen to sleep on the sofa in the living room, said that one evening he had heard the refrigerator open and other times someone banging on the sofa, but he appeared calm in front of this presence. Despite this unusual "guest", we continued to experience the Duck House as if nothing had happened, as someone who was part of the group invisibly, so much so that one day we decided to shoot the video for the song *I Want to Break Free*. The men had carefully sourced the outfits. Francesco presented himself as Fredde, in a black skirt and fuchsia sleeveless shirt. Luca as Brian in the curly wig and nightgown, looked just like him. Beppe played the part of John with the ever-present fox, and little Gabriel dressed as Rogerina with barrettes and a blonde wig made us double over with laughter. We started with backstage, makeup and accessories. The set with the antique furnishings was perfect. The stairs were missing but I had drawn them in almost real size. Everything was ready for filming. We women dressed as men as in the central part of the song. For a four-minute video, it took us two days, but the satisfaction and fun were rewarding.

We did everything to remember Freddie. It was a part not only of us, but also of that pharmacist who had filled his windows in the hall and sideways with his raised fist. And of that bar in front of the casino called *Adam's*, where a small statuette and photo behind it made you think that Freddie sometimes went to sip a cold beer during breaks. Not to mention the hotel management school, where numerous photos of Freddie could be seen through the large windows, it was no coincidence that it was named after Freddie Mercury.

As we walked down to the Place du Marchè, an orange and blue poster caught my attention with a phrase that united all these people, as Freddie had united us,

"Music is the language of emotions."

(Immanuel Kant)

We stopped right by the one who had made music a reason for living. We went to see him every day. Someone had put a necklace of sunflowers on him and someone else had hung the words on him so that he could read this poem that the rain was slowly erasing. I tried to compose the words broken in half with difficulty.

Freddie Darling, tu eclaire le monde de ton amour profond
En dépliant tes ailes, tel un papilon
Chaque jour qui passé, nous ramène à toi Darling Freddie
Ton amour immense, se rèpands du ciel au paradis.
Tel un ange de lumière;
tu dèverse ton amour du ciel à la terre.
Darling tu sais tu nous manques chaque jour che Dieu fait
Mais pourtant dans chacune de tes chansons, tu renais.
Darling! Je souhaitais par ces quelques lignes,
t'adresser ces mots, puor toi, notre Majesté
Notre darling Freddie, pour l'éternité

Anne Marie

These rhyming verses, hidden among drawings and photos hanging on Freddie's arm, represented the thoughts of all of us fans. A visit to The Studio Experience was always pleasant, because every time I discovered something new, like the cinema corner that I hadn't noticed. The photo I had put on the plexiglass in September was still there. Seeing it made me feel at home. This time we took it easy to watch and listen to everything, one more time, because we can never get enough of this place where there is so much of Queen's history.

It was time to go back to the Duck House, because Beppe had decided not to come with us, remaining alone to prepare lunch. I entered through the French window directly into the kitchen and I saw that he had his back to me. I pranked him, grabbing him by the waist and he jumped in fear. When he saw me, with an embarassing smile he said:

"He called me."

"Who? " I asked.

"I was in the kitchen putting the roast in the oven, when I heard a noise. I thought you were here, but instead I heard someone calling, hey jey or uei, something like that. I came out convinved it was you, but no one was there. I felt... I dont' know..."

Maybe he was a little scared. That presence that seemed like a good spirit came to look for us when we were alone. That same day Annarita went to her room to get her sweater because the temperatures had suddenly dropped, when she heard knocking on the wardrobe in the corridor to the rhythm of music. Thinking that some of us were there, she looked out the door, realizing that there was no one. Frightened, she went into the kitchen asking who had knocked on the cupboard, or if any of us were there. We looked each other straight in the eyes. Of course, our answer to this questions was in the negative. To defuse the situation I found the courage to joke asking her if the song was *We Will Rock You,* and he replied that it was very upbeat.

I don't know what this presence wanted to communicate to us, but I was sure it didn't want to scare or harm us.

At the end of those days it happened to me too. One afternoon I was walking along the corridor that led to one of the bathroooms, while everyone was in the room, except Pigotta who I thought was in hers, and it is precisely at that point that I heard some noises coming from there. I was sure it was her so I paid no attention. I returned after a few minutes when at the end of the corridor I saw Pigotta appears. I asked her where she had been all this time and she replied: "in the kitchen". I had a hard time believing what I had heard. I wasn't scared, just a little influenced. However, almost all the time we were together and in those moments we talked and laughed about it, because as they say, unity is strength, and this did not compromise the holiday, which was always beautiful and special.

The surprises continued with the return of the swan. I saw it as I walked up the steps. I called it. By now it bore an important name. It had come back to greet me. In the blink of an eye I was in front of it. Like that autumn of more than a year before, it came out of the water and let itself be caressed on the candid white feathers. I gave it something to eat and it looked at me straight in the eyes as if to thank, while I stared at that unmistakable black mark on its nose. There was an immediate connection between us. Then it slipped away so quiet and peaceful. It was all very beautiful.

The candles with our idol's initials burned slowly sheltered from that layer of fresh snow, which was not enough to make a snowman version of Freddie: he could only give off heat, the same heat that we sent him to the sky with a lantern, together with our names written with an indelible pen, like our frienship that grew stronger and stronger.

A cosy fireside chat
A little this, a little that
Sound of merry laughter skippin'by

A Winter's Tale (Queen, 1995)

The last night. This time I left the dedication the evening before leaving. I told Freddie everything we had done for him, but maybe he already knew. Sonia and I couldn't fall asleep. Pigotta said she felt alone in her room, so we made space for her between us, but she didn't come to sleep right away, at two o'clock a loud voice was heard emitting a long eeee coming from the same place where we had felt the presence. We looked at each other intently as if to confirm what we had heard, when it came again. I squeezed her hand to push her restlessness away and she felt asleep after a while.

I woke up next to her, who in turn tried to get the thoughts out of my head.
"I had a strange dream. Maybe the invisible man was the mad hatter", I told her.
She smiled at the idea, disregarding the last sentence. "Of course it was a weird dream, but now go and get ready. We have to leave", she reluctantly replied.
I remained fantasizing about that dream/reality, and about all the characters who had inhabited it. I wasn't at all frightened by the enthralling context in which I found myself, so much so that I thought of returning in the summer to enjoy a dip in the lake and a boat ride with my adventure companions. However, in comparing ourselves with other people who had previously stayed in the villa, we learned that no one had ever experienced such contact.
Before leaving the Duck House, as per the ritual, I threw another tricolor heart into the lake: green, white and red, the flag of Italy. If I had to continue like this, one day instead of stones I will find only hearts.

A soft snow had just covered the roofs. I could say that I lived the four seasons in Montreux. I turned to stare one last time at the symbolic house of *Made in Heaven* album, in which we were instead of Queen. Our entire journey was within this winter fairy tale.

It's a kind of magic
A Kind Of Magic (Queen)

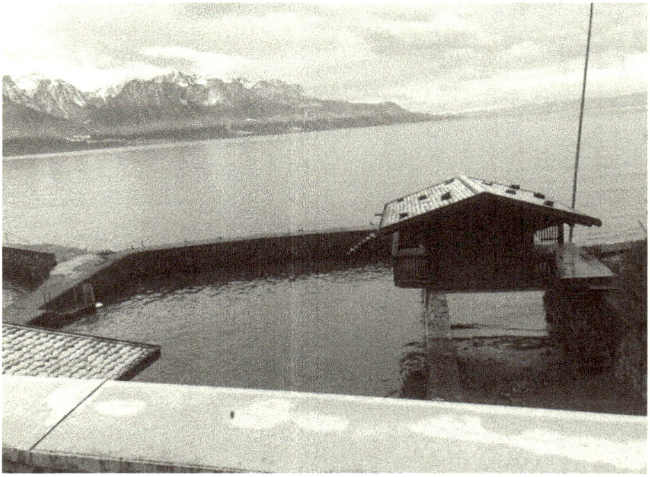

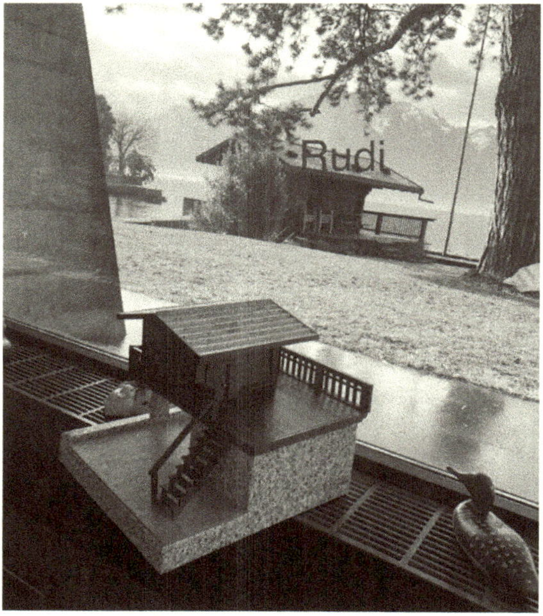
Rudi

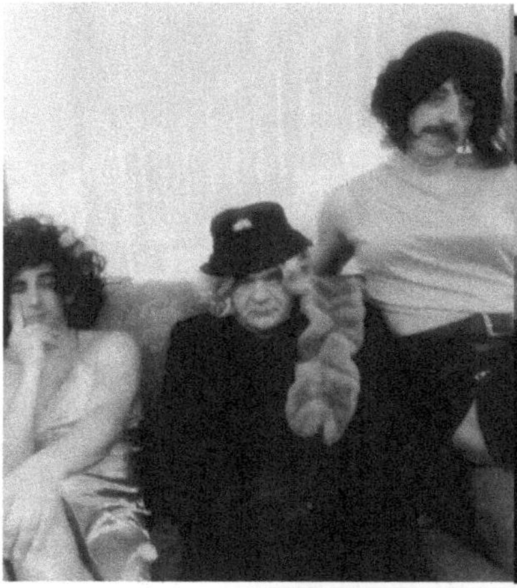
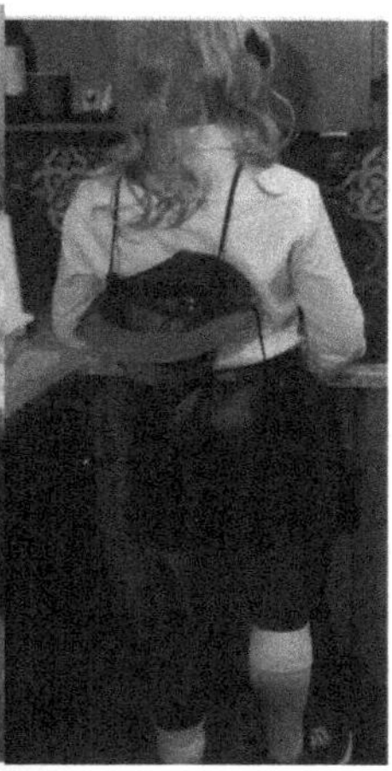

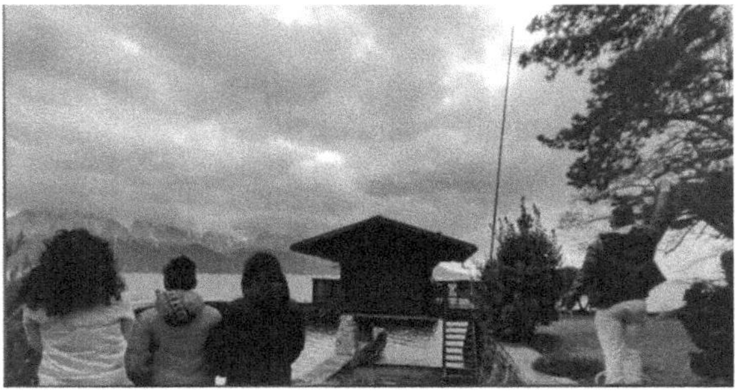

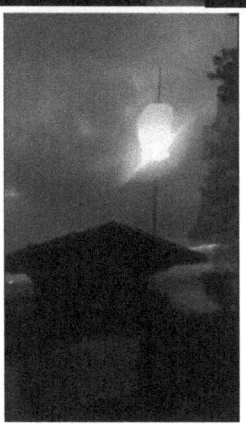

I leave you these emotions and I'm going to follow others: in Zanzibar, Japan, India, Munich, Budapest and in other parts of the world, everywhere the music of Queen and the unique and extraordinary voice of Freddie have left an indelibel imprint. Who knows if one day I will also reach the planet Mercury...

***

Being a fan is an altered state of happiness, of exuberance, of the desire to follow in the footsteps, of interest in the subject of passion and the desire to live it. All of this often leads to inspired works such as paintings or drawings (fan art), or videos (fan fiction), as led me to write this book. Being a fan means being optimistic and warm-hearted. And the beauty of feeling certain emotions that make you party, cry with joy, sing out loud, becomes essential for life. Being a fan makes you feel good, and in the end that's what we're looking for in life. Proudly the noble task of an old fan is to leave this "legacy" to the new ones, as a guarantee of the continuity of a memory that will remain alive for years to come. We have to do this for Freddie.

You loved life and lived it to the fullest, but fate had foreseen another journey for you, the one of a prince of the universe towards heaven, because perhaps your music did not reach the angels from the earth. Now you sing for them. And when you defy the laws of gravity, in the blink of an eye you come back to us and enter us with the speed of light, leaving a trail that shows the way to infinity. In your young age you have given so much, and we fans will treasure every verse of your songs, every note, every emotion. Paradoxically your short life has become our elixir of life. Instead of leaving a void, you left behind a rainbow of sounds, passions and love. You expressed the

wish that your fans would keep your music alive forever. Well yes...that music is more alive than ever in every part of the globe and is present in shows, musicals, flash mobs, through symphonies and cover bands. In stadiums your *We Are the Champions*, the rock anthem par excellence, still accompanies victories and celebrates all champions. I'm sure now you've joinded Montsy, Hendrix, George Michael, Presley, Bowie, Jackson and who knows how many others, forming a beautiful choir that reverberates across the galaxy. As an enthusiast you were able to put art into your songs, with often enigmatic but freely interpretable and philosophical lyrics, from which your expressions remain in my mind and the emotions inside me, which I have tried to free towards those who have dedicated time to read this book written in the red ink of my heart. Take them and combine them with your emotions, the magic of Queen and the magnetic effect of Freddie to make them immortal in the years to come, like their unattainable music.
I still love you.
  We still love you Freddie.
  Thanks to you I am now the music I listen to.

"Our approval is the magic that Freddie does on us and the power he has on us."

INDEX

INTRODUCTION 3

BOHEMIAN RHAPSODY, THE MOVIE (2018) 8

THE AFTER FILM 23

FREDDIE AT THE TIME OF SOCIAL 28

MONTREUX 39

STYLE AND ELEGANCE 49

AN EMOTION INSIDE EVERY SONG 54

FREDDIE IS SUPPORT, HELP AND TEACHING 66

FREDDIE BECOMES PASSION 71

SOMETHING ABOUT ME 86

AFFINITIES AND COINCIDENCES 90

FREDDIE'S PERSONALITY ACCORDING TO THE ENNEAGRAM 99

YOUR ABSENCE AND YOUR ESSENCE 108

THE GHOST TRACK 116

HOW I IMAGINE YOU TODAY 120

A WEEKEND AT THE DUCK HOUSE 126

LONDON 137

AN "UNEXPECTED" MEETING 155

THE ANNIVERSARIES 214

THE RETURN TO THE DUCK HOUSE 232

Finished printing in July 2022
Youcanprint